ANOREXIA NERVOSA:

A Survival Guide for Families, Friends, and Sufferers

Janet Treasure
Institute of Psychiatry
London, UK

R Routledge
Taylor & Francis Group
LONDON AND NEW YORK

First published 1997 by Psychology Press Ltd
27 Church Road, Hove, East Sussex BN3 2FA

Reprinted 1999 and 2000

Reprinted by Routledge 2001, 2003, 2005, 2006 and 2009
27 Church Road, Hove, East Sussex BN3 2FA
270 Madison Avenue, New York NY 10016

Routledge is an imprint of the Taylor & Francis Group, an Informa business

British Library Cataloguing in Publication Data
A catalogue record for this book is available from the British Library

ISBN 13: 978-0-86377-760-8

Cover design by Joyce Chester
Printed and bound in the UK by TJ International Ltd
This publication has been produced with paper manufactured to strict environmental standards and with pulp derived from sustainable forests.

Contents

Acknowledgements

My special thanks go to Elise Warriner who provided the illustrations at the beginning of the chapters. As always I am indebted to my husband, Tom Treasure, for providing the cartoons. Janice May has helped with the manuscript.

Finally I need to thank all clinical and research staff and patients and their relatives from the Eating Disorder Unit, Bethlem and Maudsley Trust, who have read various versions of this manuscript and have fostered the creative process. In particular I must thank Gill Todd, the nurse leader who co-ordinates all our efforts. This book was written to complement the clinical research that we are undertaking on the unit, which has been sponsored by the Mental Health Foundation and the Wellcome Trust. All royalties from this book will go towards our continuing research activities.

CHAPTER ONE

Introduction

You may be reading this because you recognise that someone you care about is suffering from anorexia nervosa. You may be confused about the illness and uncertain about how you should respond. Perhaps you feel guilty and wonder if you somehow helped to cause it. Or you may be reading this because you know you have anorexia nervosa and want to do something about it.

This book is divided into four sections. The first section gives a general outline of what anorexia is, what we believe causes it and a general historical perspective. The second section is aimed at readers who want to help understand someone they care about (daughter, son, spouse, partner, friend) who has anorexia nervosa. For convenience, however, and because most sufferers are young women, we will usually refer to "sufferers" as daughters and usually refer to the carers as parents. The third section is written for the reader with anorexia nervosa and includes strategies to cope with and hopefully overcome the illness. The fourth section is for the professional who has been asked to help. The practitioners are varied: teachers, general doctors, counsellors, social workers, psychologists and psychiatrists. However, we expect all parties to read each other's chapters. The main focus of treatment is on collaboration—working together. There are no secrets here.

A major problem in writing about anorexia nervosa is that the clinical picture is so diverse. It can range from a mild transient episode, to a life-threatening illness or a chronic debilitating condition. It can afflict young girls or mature women.

Like the curate's egg this book may therefore be good in parts. You will need to select which parts are relevant to you. It may seem strange to put the section for carers first before the section for sufferers themselves. Our justification for this is (a) that this order is appropriate in the case of the youngest sufferers, and (b) even in older sufferers it usually takes some work before they are ready and able to fight off anorexia nervosa. However, expect to miss bits out and jump from section to section rather than slavishly reading from the beginning to the end.

Anorexia nervosa is a terrifying illness which can develop insidiously in adolescents, but also at other crisis points in life. Often, parents, friends and teachers know that something is wrong but don't know what to do. Their lack of information can be paralysing. Parents may be desperate to help but afraid of seeming interfering or intrusive. Accepting that their daughter has an illness with psychological connotations may be difficult. Often parents have problems coming up with a joint plan of action because anorexia nervosa is out of the realms of their experience. Father may suggest one approach and mother another, while the anorexia nervosa continues unabated.

Similarly, teachers may spot anorexia nervosa in a pupil but find themselves at a loss as to how to help. It may be difficult for teachers to know how involved they should become. Is it appropriate for them to inform the parents? What can they do if the parents state that nothing is wrong? How can they work with parents to ensure that the anorexia nervosa doesn't take over their daughter? How can they integrate a pupil back in to school after she has had time off with anorexia nervosa?

General practitioners may be confused over the best way forward for someone suffering from anorexia nervosa. They might not always know if anorexia nervosa is the correct diagnosis. Once the diagnosis is made it may be unclear how professionals can help.

The aim of this book is to provide the necessary information about anorexia nervosa to enable those involved to recognise and address it.

Recovery *is* possible although it usually requires much hard work.

There is no doubt that the sooner the illness is recognised the easier it is to intervene to prevent it becoming a way of life.

SECTION ONE

Anorexia Nervosa: Overview

CHAPTER TWO

What is anorexia nervosa?

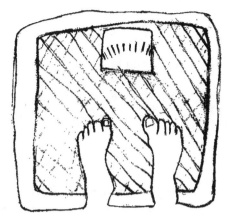

In anorexia nervosa the individual finds it extremely difficult to maintain a weight which is compatible with health. The illness is much more common in women. For those affected, gaining weight is a terrifying prospect. Sufferers have not necessarily lost their appetite. The desire to lose weight is different from that of the hunger striker, who will stop starving if his or her goals are met. Sadly, for the person with anorexia nervosa, losing weight becomes a way of life with no end point.

It may difficult to understand why such intense feelings are provoked by eating or gaining weight. Most people would find it impossible to tolerate the physical pain, distress and misery associated with starvation.

Anorexia nervosa is suffered by a diverse range of people. Some of our sufferers have led tragic lives, whereas for others, anorexia nervosa appears to be the only blot on the landscape. Here are some of their stories. Perhaps one or two will remind you of the person you know.

CASE EXAMPLES

Clare
    Clare was the middle child and had two brothers. Her older brother was bright and intense, and Clare felt that her mother focused all her academic ambitions on him. Clare believed her mother was

only interested in her daughter's appearance. As a child, Clare's mother told her she was fat and commented on how much she ate and on her shape. Clare loved sport, but because the exercise made her hungry she gave it up and concentrated on dieting. She knew her mother loved her but could not understand why she placed so much emphasis on size rather than her daughter's happiness. Clare believed that if she kept her weight down she would be contented, attractive and loved; instead she was always tired, irritable and hungry.

Stephen

Stephen had always been plump. He coped with being laughed at and scorned by becoming a comic himself. At the age of 18 he stopped eating normally when, at a consultation with his general practitioner, he was asked if there was a family history of obesity.

Joan

Joan's mother died when she was 11. She looked after herself and her father for two years until he remarried. Joan's father and stepmother immediately had a child and again Joan was left to fend for herself. She studied hard at school, but had few close friends. She moved out of her family home as soon as she could. Her stepmother encouraged her. She thought that her stepmother wanted the house to herself with no memories of her mother. Joan became a nurse, married and had a daughter. However, she developed anorexia nervosa at the time that she realised that her husband was having an affair. This made her feel alone and that she had no one to trust. Joan's parents-in-law have had to look after her daughter because she was unable to care for her daughter when she stopped eating.

Beatrice

Beatrice enjoyed school and was the centre of a small group of girls. She was very close to one girl and comments were made about whether they were in love. Beatrice's family moved when her father was promoted. She felt very lonely and unhappy. Her younger brother seemed to have no problems settling into his new school. Beatrice had always been a little overweight and people in the street used to call her "Fatty". Her mother decided to go to Weight Watchers and asked Beatrice if she wanted to go to keep her company. Beatrice went and her weight fell off. Her diet became anorexia nervosa. When she was 17 she was referred by her general practitioner for extra help. She was extremely unhappy during her first year at polytechnic but managed to complete the required credits.

Raj

Raj was the only child in an Indian family. His mother was a teacher and his father an engineer. He had always been well liked at school and was academically successful. But he wished he had a brother or sister with whom he could share experiences. Raj was one of the first boys in his class to go through puberty. He became concerned when he started having erections and some sexual fantasies involving boys. He was too shy to discuss these matters with his father or his friends. He began to eat less and to work out for many hours on his rowing machine. He found his sexual fantasies disappeared on this regime.

Joyce

Joyce came from a close, big Catholic family. She wanted her independence, and started going out with an older man when she was 16. After two years she became pregnant by him. He said Joyce should have an abortion, otherwise he would end the relationship. Joyce was shocked and horrified but went ahead with the pregnancy on her own. Her parents helped but Joyce had difficulty eating because of nausea, which has persisted, even though her son is now two years old. She became depressed and had no energy. Joyce was embarrassed by her thin appearance.

Samantha

Samantha had had episodes of depression all her life, and they had usually responded to anti-depressants from her general practitioner. This episode was different. She found it very difficult to eat. Food lay heavily on her stomach and it tended to repeat on her. She started vomiting to make herself comfortable.

Tom

Tom moved jobs and became anxious. He was concerned not to appear lazy so he increased his exercise routine and controlled his eating. His weight fell rapidly as he developed anorexia nervosa.

A variety of different explanations are offered as reasons for not eating.

Christine stopped eating at work in the belief that after lunch she was not as efficient.

Carol developed rituals about food. She could not finish eating anything. She cut her food into tiny pieces and always ate half. She began eating smaller and smaller amounts.

All *Trish* could say was that eating gave her an uncomfortable feeling in her stomach.

Kate declared herself not to be an anorexic. She felt a fraud. Despite help her weight continued to drop.

In over half of the cases of anorexia nervosa weight loss occurs as a result of exercise and a restriction of food intake. Other forms of weight control such as vomiting and taking laxatives or diet pills may also be used.

The distinction between anorexia nervosa and bulimia nervosa (bingeing alternating with starving or vomiting) is often unclear. Some sufferers from anorexia remain underweight and yet periodically gorge themselves. Mixed features of anorexia nervosa and bulimia nervosa multiply the medical problems associated with an eating disorder (see Chapter 11). Occasionally, very dangerous behaviours develop as illustrated by Paula's case.

Paula

Paula developed anorexia nervosa when she was 12 after a change of school. Her parents were keen that she had a good education and Paula was sent to a school in the next town which was academically successful. Most of her friends attended the more local school. Paula's parents became preoccupied at this time with her older sister's difficulties with a violent boyfriend. Paula's weight fell rapidly. She was admitted to hospital but begged her parents to have her discharged early. At home Paula found eating difficult and started to binge. On one occasion she took an overdose of paracetamol which led to dramatic nausea and vomiting. After this episode she regularly took 6–8 paracetamol when she felt out of control in order to experience the nausea which would stop her binge eating.

Anorexia can therefore include many different types of illness. The classic form of anorexia nervosa has been seen over several centuries, but in our current culture we are seeing a much more diverse form of illness.

UNDERSTANDING ANOREXIA

As you can see from the case examples, anorexia nervosa is a complex illness. It may be impossible for people with normal appetites to understand what is happening. One image that can be helpful is to imagine a separate anorexia "minx" sitting on your daughter's shoulder, whispering false information into her ear.

SEEKING HELP

Although the aim of this book is to provide you with information and ideas about ways that you can help, anorexia nervosa can often be a severe illness with life-threatening complications, or may become very entrenched and last five years or more. In many cases, professional help is needed. Medical problems arise because of starvation and these need to be assessed by a doctor.

One of the first steps is to go to your general practitioner, he or she will discuss with you what additional help is required and will know how to access the necessary medical and psychological help. In some cases, intensive psychological help is required. Families are often seen together as they can play a major role in helping their daughter overcome the illness.

Anorexia nervosa is quite a rare illness. The sense of isolation and loneliness which occurs when you face the problem makes things worse. Making contact with others with the same problem can help. The Eating Disorders Association is an excellent resource for getting this help. You can get information and regular newsletters by post if you write to them. Their address is: Eating Disorders Association, Sackville Place, 44–48 Magdalen Street, Norwich, Norfolk NR3 1JE. They provide telephone help-lines, and also support a network of self-help groups throughout the country. They also provide support groups for parents.

CHAPTER THREE

Who or what is to blame?

Anorexia nervosa throws families into confusion. Living with someone with anorexia nervosa can be very difficult, as the sufferer's behaviour may seem to be deliberately provocative and selfish. At times like this it can be hard to remember that anorexia is an expression of unhappiness and distress. Families may torment themselves wondering "where did we go wrong?". There are no simple explanations and this is an inappropriate question.

The sufferer is also very confused. On one level she can hear others begging her to snap out of it and just eat but on another level this is one thing that she cannot do even if her life depends on it.

The illness often arises out of a complex mixture of many factors. It is easier to draw up a list of what anorexia nervosa is not rather than suggest what it is:

- It is not an indication that parents have gone badly wrong bringing up their child.
- It is not a phase of silly, stubborn naughtiness.
- Nor is it something that sufferers can "just snap out of".

Having anorexia nervosa is a wretched, lonely experience but it is not a modern phenomenon. If we go back to historical medical records we find that young women and some young men have had an illness remarkably like modern anorexia nervosa over the last four centuries

(Chapter 4 deals with this in more detail). Although there is no overwhelming evidence that anorexia nervosa is increasing in frequency in modern times, what we do find is evidence that it is becoming more difficult to overcome when it does arise. Our present culture with its emphasis on thinness tends to lock people into a career of anorexia nervosa.

We will attempt to outline some of the various facets which appear to lead to anorexia nervosa. No one mechanism is responsible, instead several smaller things, which in isolation are innocuous, but together with other factors appear to precipitate the problem.

THE CULTURE OF THINNESS

Fashion

Some cultures predispose to anorexia nervosa. Our present Western culture may increase the risk with its emphasis on thinness, skeletal super models, and dieting behaviour as a norm for young women.

There has been an increase in the number of young women presenting with anorexia nervosa and the illness is striking younger people as time passes. However, this increase in anorexia nervosa is not as marked as in bulimia nervosa.

Anorexia nervosa is less likely to be a "slimming disease" than bulimia nervosa. Clearly, however, a slimming culture perpetuates the problem. In some cases career choice exaggerates the need to be slim as happened with Sarah.

Sarah

Sarah was training at drama school to be an actress. Her tutor drew her aside and said that she would need to control her weight as television work led to everybody looking bigger on the screen than they were. She immediately went on a diet and her weight fell. Once she returned home to her parents they had to take her to the doctor because she could hardly walk upstairs and found brushing her hair difficult. She was immediately admitted to hospital.

Mastery

Thinness is often regarded as a sign of mastery and self-control (regardless of how the control of body weight is achieved). This fashion for thinness is no different to any other cultural ideal of female beauty. For example, the bound "lotus" feet of Chinese women were thought to be desirable. In fact they crippled women and led to chronic pain, and ill health. (Read further about this in the novel *Wild swans* by Jung Chang.) It is important to put this fashion for thinness into context. (See Chapter 12 for further details about nutrition, weight and body composition.)

Health

One message transmitted by the media is "the lower the weight, the better the health". This is *not true*. For mature women, the lowest levels of mortality are associated with a weight above what is regarded as the "normal" range. Also, the typical female pear-shaped distribution of fat, with a thin waist and rounded hips and thighs is not associated with any metabolic complications. Instead, the waist/hip ratio rather than weight is a better marker of risk, with the lower the ratio the better. A ratio of 0.75 is typical for women, a ratio of greater than 1 is associated with various health risks.

Messages about diet and health are aimed at middle-aged men who have the highest risk of heart disease. Extremely low fat diets may not be heathy, especially if they are used with other so-called healthy combinations, such as a no sugar or carbohydrate diet.

Fear of food

Advice about healthy eating often becomes confused with the idea that certain foodstuffs such as sugars and fats are bad. Scientific knowledge is incomplete and there are large swings in fashion. Twenty years ago carbohydrates were considered to be "bad". The pendulum has swung and carbohydrates are now "good" whereas fats are "bad". The diet that is perceived to be "good" may not have enough calories and so leads to intolerable hunger and an overwhelming need to break the rules. To the best of our knowledge it makes sense to aim to have a diet which has less that 50% fat. Generally speaking, there is no such thing as "bad" or "unhealthy" food, simply a more or less healthy balance of foods.

Food is now regarded with suspicion and fear. We are bombarded with warnings about salmonella, listeria, BSE, cholesterol, animal fats and sugar. This may mean that individuals who have a risk for compulsive worries about dangers that they may be responsible for, who in the past would have been plagued with fears of contamination from germs or disasters through not controlling power supplies, etc., may now be preoccupied with the dangers that food contains and have joined the wider group of eating disorders.We find that many people who now have anorexia nervosa also have problems with obsessive compulsive disorders. As children they may have had a compulsion to do specific behaviour such as touching to ward off perceived danger.

A backlash is developing against the culture of thinness. Programmes have been developed in Norway and the United States with the aim of counteracting the forces of the dieting industry. One example of their activity is to ban an advert for a cola drink which included a dieting competition for teenagers. In the United Kingdom, the Independent Television Commission has drawn up rules about advertising slimming products.

IT'S ALL IN THE FAMILY, OR IS IT?

Families often feel compelled to find the cause of the illness and spend a lot of time going over the past, blaming themselves and feeling guilty. Although it is important to let your doctor or therapist know about any family or other difficulties that you think might be relevant, there is no point in blaming yourself; this will not help anyone get better. The past needs to be accepted, mistakes and successes equally, and energy concentrated on the present and recovery.

It is common for parents to feel torn in two. First, you see your daughter locked into behaviour that is causing her more and more problems, and then you may question whether the way you have handled problems and stresses in the past has been a factor in the development of her anorexia. Your questions may stop you trying to help. Do not let this negative thinking inhibit you. Your help is needed and is critical for your daughter's health.

Much work has been done to try and understand the causes of eating disorders. None of the research shows great differences in family functioning between families with an anorexia nervosa sufferer and those without. The conclusion is that *families are not to blame*.

Research has found that in some ways, families of patients with anorexia nervosa resemble those with a child with cystic fibrosis. This suggests that the presence of a severely ill child affects family function, rather than family functioning "causing" a child to be ill. A severely ill child causes parents to become protective. It brings out an instinctive response to try to shield your daughter from outside pressures and to discourage her from trying to stand on her own two feet. Unfortunately, problems with psychological components impinge on all areas of life. Anorexia nervosa cannot be cured by pills or an operation. It is an illness that has to be struggled with over several years. It is for these reasons that families are often invited to help in the treatment of their daughter. It is not a matter of finding the culprit or the secret but rather one of working as a team with the sufferer to help fight off the stranglehold of anorexia.

GENETIC RISK

There does appear to be a genetic risk to developing anorexia nervosa. For example, a mother, grandmother or aunt may have also had the illness. It is not uncommon to have more than one affected member in the immediate family, whereas the illness is quite rare in the general population. In a study of twins from the Maudsley Hospital we found that it was common for both members of sets of identical twins to have the illness whereas if the twins were not identical it was usual for anorexia nervosa to be present in only one twin. Some vulnerability, we do not know what it is, runs in families. The vulnerability can come from either the maternal or paternal lines.

Jenny

Jenny developed anorexia nervosa at the age of 17. The family realised that her illness resembled what had happened to her grandmother at the age of 15 in 1935. Her grandmother had lost weight when she was a schoolgirl. Her weight had fallen from 8 stone to 5 stone. The doctor had found nothing wrong with Jenny's grandma that could explain her weight loss. The doctor and the family were worried and so Jenny's grandma was admitted to a nursing home where she gradually gained weight after the nurses were able to persuade her to eat.

If we look to the wider animal kingdom we see that not only are food preferences and body composition under genetic control, but there are also conditions that resemble anorexia nervosa. Young female pigs of certain stocks can suffer from a condition called "thin sow syndrome". Female pigs from these lines become locked into irretrievable emaciation. Their behaviour is similar to that seen in anorexia nervosa. They show a preference for low energy feed (straw). They become hyperactive and infertile. Lines of pigs that have been bred for leanness are particularly at risk. However, the problem is triggered by stress. In the case of pigs this stress is caused by separating sow and piglets too early and expecting them to adjust to new peer relationships.

We can conclude that some families have a constitution which puts members at risk of developing anorexia nervosa. However, many other factors contribute to the onset and maintenance of the disorder.

WHAT ARE THE TRIGGERS?

Stresses such as deaths or disappointments can trigger the illness particularly in the context of certain personality features. It can be useful to know what these triggers are as anorexia nervosa may have developed as a way of coping with the event. However, anorexia nervosa leads to avoidance of the problem rather than finding an effective way of dealing with it. It may be possible and necessary to process the event in a more adaptive way.

Stephen
> Stephen was away at an all-boys boarding school. He had been slightly plump before puberty but as his growth accelerated he became very tall and lean. He became very interested in cross country running and was successful at this. However, Stephen developed a hip problem which gave him severe pain. He went to the doctor and was told that he would have to give up running. The pain continued and he had to have an operation. Stephen was very upset about this as running had been one of his major sources of pleasure. At about the same time he developed an ulcer on his penis. He was too embarrassed to go to the matron at school to talk about this problem and so soldiered on for several days. Stephen eventually told his mother who arranged for him to see a general practitioner. He needed to have surgery. Afterwards he became very withdrawn and his mood fell. Stephen didn't enjoy the company of the other boys and felt unable to take part in the to-and-fro repartee that characterised schoolboy banter. He became obsessed with his weight and appearance. He started to avoid school meals and became preoccupied with fitness. He went on a variety of diets. He bought slimming books. His weight fell and his parents took him to his general practitioner who referred him to a psychiatrist.

Issues in Stephen's treatment were to consider the blows to his self-esteem caused by the inability to run and the painful embarrassment caused by the ulcer. He was able to discuss and explore these in therapy without worrying about appearing a wimp or needing to keep a stiff upper lip. He was able to express his sadness and frustration that he would no longer be able to run. Using problem-solving strategies he considered other activities which would give him pleasure and mastery but which would not put stress on his legs. He decided to take up rowing. During the revision time for his

A-levels he was able to stay at home. At home he was surrounded by support and love, rather than teasing and competitiveness. He found it much easier to eat at home. During the course of therapy he grew 5cm and gained another 20kg over several months.

Susan

Susan developed anorexia nervosa after the death of her grandfather. She had been particularly close to him as they shared many interests. He would take Susan on fishing trips every weekend. She looked upon him almost as a father as her own father was frequently out of the house. Susan's parents had never got on well. It was difficult for her to grieve for her grandfather as she felt that she had to be strong to look after her mother who had more right to grieve and be upset than she.

Part of the work of therapy was to grieve and come to terms with the loss of an important figure in her life. This was a long process of acknowledging the love and care that she had from her grandfather and, as a consequence the loneliness and misery caused by his death. Part of the normal grief response is to feel anger at the loved one for going. People with anorexia nervosa often find it difficult to accept that they can be angry with people they love and so they block off this feeling. This prevents the normal emotional processing from taking place and the sufferer remains stuck as if the loss had just happened. Tears will spill out when talking about the event years later.

Another case in which there were obvious triggers was that of Margaret.

Margaret

Margaret had trained to be a nurse and had a good job in a London teaching hospital. Her mother developed breast cancer and it fell to Margaret to help care for her. She had to do this as well as her ordinary job and became exhausted. Once or twice her professionalism slipped and she became irritated. To her horror once or twice she snapped at her mother. Margaret was with her mother when she died, and although she knew it was hopeless, tried to resuscitate her. She appeared calm and collected at the funeral looking after her father and her sister. She didn't cry or break down herself, but carried on supporting her father over the next few months. At the same time her weight began to fall. Obviously the death of her mother and her difficulty in grieving her loss were important issues dealt with in treatment.

It must be emphasised that this work is not all plain sailing. Once Margaret started to gain weight she became very anxious. She became plagued by nightmares in which she relived the events of her mother's death. At times she was almost tempted to stop eating again as though this would make it all go away.

WHAT ARE THE PERSONAL CHARACTERISTICS THAT PUT PEOPLE AT RISK?

Perfectionism in at least one sphere of life, whether that be tidiness, academic success or athletic prowess, is a risk factor. It is almost as if the sufferer's drive for perfection is to appease a self-critical part of themselves. The perfectionism therefore does not give pleasure but wards off pain. Central to the drive to attain perfection is a low opinion of the self.

This fragile sense of self is associated with a strong drive to seek the approval of others. Extreme external yardsticks of success or achievement are used. For example, getting the top mark or exhibiting immense stamina in exercise training. You may have noticed these traits in your daughter. However, once the eating disorder appears, perhaps for the first time in her life, your daughter will become angry and stubborn in her insistence that she continues in her anorexic behaviour. She may no longer try to please or smooth things over at home.

Another personality streak is one which values control over normal instincts and pleasures. This is the sort of personality that advocates the puritanical or selfless spirituality associated with asceticism in religion. In some people it may come across as stubbornness. It includes the beliefs that if you work hard you can overcome a problem, and that there is moral worth in trying to suppress or overcome your nature including your need for food. Unfortunately, this characteristic, when combined with the "Protestant work ethic" culture, can lead to setting unrealistic goals. These personality factors are dealt with in more detail in Chapter 13.

The way people with anorexia nervosa cope with problems can be self-defeating. They may feel more helpless about the problem, more pessimistic about its outcome and may blame themselves in some way. Sufferers might blame themselves for bringing on the problem or criticise themselves for feeling unhappy. These responses seem to reflect a belief that "If I have a problem, I am bad/imperfect" or "If I can't solve my problem straight away then I must be inadequate". Clearly, these beliefs are triggered by the occurrence of problems and are at odds with the desire to be perfect.

This wish for perfection and control and the belief that they are unobtainable or unworthy in some way, may also prevent people with anorexia nervosa from opening up to someone and talking about their difficulties. The ability to trust others is impaired. Obtaining this kind of emotional support is known to be a factor that protects people against developing psychological problems.

It may be that the development of an eating disorder in your own daughter cannot be explained by any of these aspects. We are aware that our current models cannot explain everything. We would be interested to hear about your theories. Perhaps you can write to us with them.

FURTHER READING

Chang, Jung. (1991). *Wild swans*. London: HarperCollins.

Books that challenge the dieting culture:

Katzman, M.A., & Wooley, S. (1994). *Feminist perspectives on eating disorders*. New York: Guilford Press.
Ogdon, J. (1990). *Fat chance. The myth of dieting explained*. London: Routledge.
Sanders, T., & Bazalgette, P. (1993). *You don't have to diet*. London Bantam.
Wolf, N. (1990). *The beauty trap*. London: Vintage.

CHAPTER FOUR

Ferment in the feminals: Time and time again

One of the most difficult things about coping with anorexia nervosa is the feeling of isolation and confusion. Despite the media interest few of us really know what it is like to be, or to live with someone who is struggling with the illness. It is unusual to know another family who has the same problem. Families are full of questions. What is happening to us? What should we do about it? Why has this happened to us? What did we do that was wrong? You may fear that it is your family's unique shortcomings which have led to the problem. We hope that after reading Chapter 3 you do not blame yourselves.

It may be helpful to know that you are not alone. Not only are there other families who share your concerns but this problem has been around for centuries. The case examples from the past can help identify how much of the difficulties you are experiencing result from anorexia nervosa rather than individual quirks and querulousness. We will also review how the approach to treatment has evolved over time.

HISTORICAL BACKGROUND

Richard Morton (1694) is usually credited with the first medical description of patients with anorexia nervosa. In his book on wasting illnesses *Phthisiologia or a Treatise of consumptions*, he describes two patients whose illness appeared to be due to voluntary food restriction:

Mr Duke's daughter in St Mary Axe, in the year 1684, and the eighteenth year of her age, in the month of July fell into a total suppression of her Monthly Courses from a multitude of Cares and Passions ... From which time her appetite began to abate and her digestion to be bad; her flesh also began to be flaccid and loose and her looks pale ... she was wont by her studying at night and continuing pouring upon Books to expose herself both day and night to the injuries of the air ... From that time loathing all sorts of medicaments she wholly neglected the care of herself for two full years, till at last brought to the last degree of a marasmus, or consumption, and thereupon subject to frequent fainting fits, she applied herself to me for advice.

I do not remember that I did ever, in all my practice, see one that was conversant with the Living, so much wasted ... she was like a Skeleton only clad with skin, yet there was no fever but on the contrary a coldness of the whole body; no cough or difficulty with breathing nor another distemper of the lungs or of any other entrail. Only her appetite was diminished and her Digestion uneasy, with fainting fits which did frequently return upon her. Which symptoms I did endeavour to relieve by the outward application of Aromatic Bags made to the region of the Stomack and by Stomack-Plaiters, as also by the internal use of bitter Medicine, Chalybeates and Juleps made of Cephalick and Antihysterick Waters, sufficiently impregnated with Spirit of salt Armoniack and Tincture of Castor ... but being quickly tired with medicines she beg'd that the whole affair might be committed again to nature whereupon consuming every day more and more, she was after three months taken with a fainting fit and dyed.

The second patient Morton described was a 16-year-old son of a church minister who:

fell gradually into a total want of appetite, occasioned by studying too hard and the Passions of the Mind ... pining away more and more for a space of two years. This consumption was nervous and had its seat in the whole habit of the body.

This case was cured by advice which was to:

abandon his studies, to go into the country air, and to use riding and a milk diet.

Another probable case of anorexia nervosa was Martha Taylor. She was a young girl from Derbyshire who ate no solid food for 12–13 months and lost so much weight that "part of her belly touches her backbones". She was visited by nobility and by several physicians. John Reynolds went to visit her on behalf of the Royal Society. He produced a report (1669) describing her case and those of others that he knew of. He speculated on the cause of this phenomenon:

> Most of these Demoiselles fall to this abstinence between the age of fourteen and twenty years. Tis probably that the feminal humours in these virgins may be a long abode in their vessels grow acid. Her Age confirms the probability of a ferment in the feminals.

Unequivocal medical descriptions of anorexia nervosa appeared in the 19th century. Marcé, a young French psychiatrist, wrote in 1860 of:

> young girls who at the period of puberty become subject to inappetancy carried to the utmost limited ... these patients arrive at the delirious conviction that they cannot or ought not to eat ... All attempts made to constrain them to adopt a sufficient regimen are opposed with infinite strategies and unconquerable resistance. This behaviour persists until all traces of adipose tissue has disappeared and the patients are reduced to skeletons. They develop a weakness so great that they could scarcely walk a few steps. These unhappy patients only regain some amount of energy in order to resist attempts at alimentation ... Some literally die of hunger but medical intervention can be most advantageous even when the patient seems devoted to incurability and death. I have seen three young girls thus cured who were reduced to a most alarming and almost desperate state. I would venture to say that the first physicians who attended the patients misunderstood the true significance of this obstinate refusal of food: far from seeing in it a delirious idea of a hypochondriacal nature, they occupied themselves solely with the state of the stomach.

Sir William Gull (a physician at Guy's Hospital) and Charles Lasegue (a French psychiatrist) between 1868 and 1888 brought the illness to the attention of the medical community with articles and case presentations.

Lasegue's account is particularly vivid and well observed. He describes the lack of insight into the dangerousness of the weight loss and details all the excuses and reasons used to explain the refusal to eat.

At first the patient feels uneasiness after meals, a vague sensation of fullness. The same sensations are repeated during the course of several days. They may be slight, but they are tenacious. She feels that the best remedy for this indefinite discomfort will be to diminish her food intake. As yet there is nothing remarkable in her case. But gradually she reduces her food further and further and furnishes pretexts for so doing ... By the end of a few weeks, there is no longer a temporary repugnance, but a refusal of food that may be indefinitely prolonged. The disease has declared itself ... Meal after meal is discontinued and almost always some article of diet is successively suppressed.

Sometimes one food is replaced by another for which an exclusive predilection may be manifested. At first the general health does not appear to be aversely affected, and the constipation readily yields to mild laxatives. The abstinence tends to increase the aptitude for movement. The patient feels lighter and more active. She is able to pursue a tiring day without being aware of the lassitude of which she would at other times have complained. Both her family and her medical attendants become increasingly concerned, and the anorexia gradually becomes the sole preoccupation and topic of conversation. The patient no longer troubles herself to find an excuse for not eating. When told she cannot possibly live on the amount of food that would not suffice for an infant she replies that it furnishes sufficient nourishment for her adding that she had never refused to undertake any task or labour. She knows better than anyone what she requires, moreover it would be impossible for her to tolerate a more abundant diet ... she says that she never was in better health and suffers in no way 'I do not suffer and therefore I must be well' is the monotonous formula which has replaced 'I cannot eat because I am unwell'. In fact the whole disease is summed up in this intellectual perversion.

Eventually, the tolerance of her economy, marvellous though it may be, is exhausted. The disease enters upon its third stage. Extreme emaciation occurs, general debility increases and exercise becomes laborious. The patient may now allow some refeeding, but grudgingly with the evident hope that she will avert her peril without renouncing her ideas and perhaps the interest that her malady has inspired ... I know patients who even ten years after the onset of their illness have not yet recovered the aptitude of eating like other people.

John Ryle a physician from Guy's Hospital, London, gave the Schorstein Lecture in 1936, which was later published in the *Lancet*. He presented his experience of 51 cases of anorexia nervosa seen over 16 years. He gave 8 case histories to illustrate the various forms of the illness.

These descriptions are for the benefit of doctors and describe the physical symptoms. This is the first case he describes:

Case 1

A girl aged 19 had been healthy and jolly in childhood, worked hard at school, matriculating at 16, and six months before went to France to learn the language. Just before she left home her periods previously regular stopped and she began to eat poorly. From that time she became steadily thinner. Except for things containing vinegar and salads she had a dislike for all good food. Her mother was very worried and they clearly "got on each others nerves". She was quiet and conscientious and liked her work in a bank. She complained of no symptoms. At home she was said to be happy as a rule, but sometimes nervy and irritable and apt to cry over the attempts to make her eat. Weight formerly 8st 10 lb now 6st 9 lb. Small undeveloped downy hair on face arms and back, blotchy red hands. Pulse 80 blood pressure 95/75. Treating at home in bed for a month her doctor secured a gain of 1.5 lb but the improvement was not sustained. In five months following the consultation again with home treatment after full explanation to the mother she gained 1st in weight. She then went back to her work and in the six subsequent years she never missed a day. Menstruation became normal within two months of the second course of treatment She is now married and happy and has a healthy baby. Peripheral circulation remains poor.

These examples over three centuries apart have remarkable similarities to the way anorexia nervosa presents today. Not only is food refusal and extreme starvation a consistent feature but over-activity either physical or academic is an integral feature. A major difference from cases of today is that in none of these is fear of fatness or the pursuit of thinness given as a reason for not eating.

TIME TRENDS IN TREATMENT

One of the difficult aspects of anorexia nervosa is that there is no simple medical treatment such as a drug or an operation. Treatment has developed empirically based on clinical observation of what works. It is therefore of interest to note how treatment has developed over time and what the outcome and prognosis was and to compare it with treatment and outcome now.

Most of the authors who describe cases also discussed treatment. Richard Morton's (1694) advice was:

> Let the patient endeavour to divert and make his mind cheerful by exercise, and the conversation of his friends. For this disease does almost always proceed from Sadness and Anxious Cares. Let him also enjoy the benefit of an open, clear and very good Air, which does very much relieve the nerves and spirits. And because the Stomach in this Distemper is principally affected a delicious diet will be convenient, and the Stomach ought not to be long accustomed to one sort of food.

Marcé (1860) was struck by how difficult it was to implement treatment at home, he therefore advised:

> The hypochondriacal delirium, then, cannot be advantageously encountered so long as the subjects remain in the midst of their own family and their habitual circle: the obstinate resistance that they offer, the sufferings of the stomach, which they enumerate with incessant lamentation, produce too vivid an emotion to admit of the physician acting with full liberty and obtaining the necessary moral ascendancy. It is therefore indispensable to change the habitation and the surrounding circumstances and to entrust the patients to the care of strangers.
>
> It is necessary to proceed progressively and by degrees. Each day at each repast the nourishment be it liquid or solid, should be gradually increased. As to exercise and gymnastics, which are commonly recommended, they have the inconvenience of a great expenditure of energy, which the daily alimentation is unable to withstand. These patients will be seen to undergo a great change and their strength and condition to return and their intellectual state to be modified in a most striking manner...but relapses are in these cases easy.

Gull's (1874) advice was very similar. He also acknowledged that it was important not to lose sight of the primary goal of treatment which is to restore adequate nutrition by not succumbing to the sufferer's explanations and protestations. He was confident that the problem lay in the mind and that the patient's reasoning and logic was at fault:

In reference to treatment the patients require moral control: and that, if possible a change in domestic relations should be made. From the beginning food should be given at short intervals and that patients should not be left to their own inclination in the matter. The inclination of the patients must in no way be consulted. In earlier and less severe cases it is not unusual for the medical attendant to say in reply to the anxious solicitude of the parents, 'Let her do as she like. Don't force food'. Formerly I thought such advice admissible and proper but larger experience has shown plainly the danger of allowing the starvation process to go on … patients should be fed at regular intervals and surrounded by persons who would have moral control over them: relatives and friends being generally the worst attendants.

As regards prognosis, none of these cases, however exhausted are really hopeless whilst life exists, and for the most part the prognosis may be considered favourable. The restless activity referred to is also to be controlled but this is often difficult.

Gull illustrated his paper with a case example of a girl, Miss C, 15 years 8 months whom he had been asked to see. His notes state:

C ailing for a year and become extremely emaciated … Very sleepless for six months hence … Lower extremities oedematous. Mind weakened. Temper obstinate. Great restlessness.

Gull wrote to her doctor advising him on her management:

Dear Dr Andersen,

I saw Miss C today. The case appears to be an extreme instance of what I have proposed to call Apepsia hysterican or Anorexia Nervosa … I would advise warm clothing, and some form of nourishing food every two hours as milk, cream, soup, eggs, fish or chicken. I must only urge the necessity of nourishment in some form otherwise the venous obstruction which had already begun to show itself by oedema of the legs will go on plugging off the vessels. With the nourishment I would conjoin a dessert spoonful of brandy every two or three hours. Whilst the present state of weakness continues, fatigue must be limited and if the exhaustion continues the patient should be kept in a warm bed …

Yours truly,

Gull obtained a letter from her doctor 6 months later reporting on progress:

Dear Sir William,
    Miss C is at Shanklin but returns soon.
    The great difficulty was to keep her quiet, and to make her eat and drink. Every step had to be fought. She was most loquacious and obstinate, anxious to exert herself bodily and mentally.

The last report was one year later:

Dear Sir William,
    I am sure you will be delighted to hear that Miss C in whose case you were so kindly interested has now made a complete recovery and is getting plump and rosy as of yore.

In the 1890s, Pierre Janet, an eminent French psychiatrist wrote of the difficulties in managing these cases. He followed Lasegue and conceptualised the illness in three phases. He called the first a gastric phase in which everyone assumes that there is an affliction of the stomach. He however notes that this first phase is more often the consequence of an emotion. The second phase is when the family become alarmed:

Now they try to allure the patient by all possible delicacies of the table, they scold her severely, they alternately spoil, beseech, threaten her. The excess of the insistence causes an exaggeration of the resistance; the girl seems to understand that the least concession on her part would cause her to pass from the condition of a patient to that of a capricious child, and to this she will never consent.
    All the relatives and friends interfere by turns to try what their authority and influence may do. The girl repeats that she is never hungry, that she does not need more food, that she can live indefinitely in that way, that, moreover she has never felt better … our strange patient struggles with all those around her by every possible means. She seeks a support in one of her parents against the other, she promises to do wonders if her family are not too exacting, she has recourse to every artifice and every untruth …

The third phase was when physical problems developed. He suggested that a proportion became frightened at this and would begin to eat but he notes that a subgroup continue to refuse to eat even at this terminal phase.
    Janet was fascinated by the refusal to eat and by the overactivity that he recognised as part of the condition. He did not think that the

overactivity was a secondary feature, rather he thought that a core feature of anorexia nervosa was a strange feeling of happiness, an euphoria in which state the need for food, feelings of weakness and depression disappeared.

John Ryle did not insist that the sufferer from anorexia nervosa had to be separated from her home surroundings. Rather, he suggested that good results can be obtained at home: "if the situation is clearly and fairly explained to the patients and (especially in the case of the younger subjects) to the parents also, and if co-operation with the family doctor is maintained by them". He goes on to state that it is useful to explain to the patients and parents separately the nature of the disease in the simplest and most direct terms. A strong assurance should be given that recovery will take place once the starvation habit is corrected and the appetite restored by giving the stomach a sufficient intake of nourishing food to maintain, not only the bodily requirements, but also its own efficiency, of which appetite is a normal expression. The absence of organic disease must be confidently expressed. Parent and child must be allowed to see that the physician has a complete grasp of the situation.

If the programme initiated at home is not proceeding satisfactorily, treatment is better carried out in a nursing home. Doctor and nurse must obtain early and full control over the patient and from the beginning ensure that the food provided is eaten. In some cases it may be necessary to sit with the patients until each meal is finished. Firmness, kindness and tact must be used in just proportions and the nurse must never let herself be wheedled into concessions. A mixed diet from the beginning is preferable. It should be remembered that some patients are capable not only of declining food but also of hiding and disposing of it and even of inducing vomiting when the nurse's back is turned. Direct inquiries into motive and difficulties are better avoided, at any rate in the earlier stages and in the youthful cases. Explanation, reassurance, distraction and firm treatment of the starvation are usually adequate and will ensure a steady and parallel improvement in the mental and physical states. Not uncommonly, a waywardness or periodic emotionalism or a subdued or alternatively a bossy attitude of mind persists after physical recovery but this is hardly to be regarded as a continuation of the disease.

Hilda Bruch was a psychoanalyst in America who developed a special interest in anorexia nervosa. She also emphasised the need to address the starvation as a priority. In the Founders Award Lecture for the American Psychiatric Association Meeting in 1981 (Bruch, 1982) she charted the development of her ideas. She had been struck by the fact that traditional psychoanalysis was rather ineffective. She ascribed part of the treatment difficulties to polarised models of treatment. She contrasted those that concentrated on weight gain only with complete disregard of the psychological problems with psychoanalysis extending over several years with disregard for the low weight.

> For effective treatment, changes and corrections must be accomplished in several areas. The patient's nutrition must be improved, the tight involvement with the family needs to be resolved and the inner confusion and misconceptions require clarification. The patient's persistent malnutrition creates psychological problems that are biologically not psychodynamically determined ... The fact is that no true picture of the psychological problems can be formulated, nor can psychotherapy be effective, until the worst malnutrition is corrected and the patient becomes capable of assimilating and processing new information.

Bruch developed a method of treatment which involved active collaboration between patient and therapist. She first explained her conceptualisation of the illness.

> The preoccupation with eating and weight is a cover up for underlying problems and patients' doubt about their self worth and value, that they need help to discover their good qualities and assets and that at this stage the severe starvation interferes with their psychological processes. It is important to clarify from the outset that the goal of psychotherapy is to accomplish something for the patient's benefit and not to appease the parents.
> In a way, all anorectic patients have to build up a new personality after all the years of fake existence. They are eternally preoccupied with the image they create in the eyes of others, always questioning whether they are worthy of respect ... There is a basic mistrust which permeates all relationships—the conviction that all people look down on them with scorn and criticism and that they have to protect themselves against this. This mistrust is usually hidden from the therapist under the facade of pleasing co-operation, at least initially. Sooner or later this will be succeeded by criticism and negativism and then by open hostility.

You can see from this brief history of treatment that the approach we have outlined in this book follows from that advocated by these luminaries in the field. One of the main tenets of treatment was for the doctor to share with the patient and the family his/her understanding of the illness and then to help them withstand the difficulties they would encounter correcting the malnutrition. Although they all understood the psychological underpinnings of the condition they also realised that they had to attend to the physical aspects of the illness as a priority. We hope that the information and suggestions that we give you in this book will build on Hilda Bruch's concept of active collaboration. For active collaboration, people with anorexia nervosa need information and help. It is difficult in a book, however, to tailor the information to suit each individual. Therefore, some parts of the book will seem too technical, some parts will seem obvious and yet others will be irrelevant. I suggest that you look through the whole text and focus on areas that are helpful and skip those that are not applicable.

FURTHER READING

Bruch, H. (1982). *Anorexia nervosa: Therapy and theory*. New York: American Psychiatric Association.

Gull, W.W. (1868). The address in medicine. Delivered before the annual meeting of the British Medical Association at Oxford. *Lancet, 2*, 171–176.

Gull, W.W. (1874). Anorexia nervosa (apepsia hysterica, anorexia hysterica). *Transactions of the Clinical Society of London, 7*, 22–28.

Janet, P. (1903). *The major symptoms of hysteria* (pp.227–244). London: Macmillan.

Lasegue, E.C. (1873). De l'anorexie hysterique. *Archives Générale de Médecine, 21*, 385–403.

Marcé, L.V. (1860). On a form of hypochondriachal delirium occurring consecutive to dyspepsia and characterised by refusal of food. *Journal of Psychological Medicine and Mental Patholody, 13*, 264–266.

Morton, R. (1694). *Phthisiologia, or A treatise of consumptions*. London: Smith and Walford.

Reynolds, J. (1669). "A discourse on prodigious abstinence". Quoted in J.A. Silverman (1986) Anorexia nervosa in seventeenth-century England as viewed by physician, philosopher and pedagogue. *International Journal of Eating Disorders, 5*, 847–853.

Ryle, J.A. (1936). *Anorexia nervosa*. Lancet, ii, 893–899.

SECTION TWO
For carers

CHAPTER FIVE

Acknowledging the problem

Relatives are faced with one of the most difficult steps in the management of anorexia nervosa—persuading the sufferer to acknowledge that she has a problem. People with anorexia nervosa frequently deny that anything is wrong and reject offers of help. Often, by the time they admit that they have a problem the illness has a stranglehold on their lives, with serious effects on their physical and psychological health, social life and career or education. At this stage, recovering is difficult. It is therefore worth considering how you can help at an early stage.

Some families have difficulty finding the correct balance between enabling their adolescent to gain independence, and helping them when difficulties arise. Families do, however, need to be involved if a member has anorexia nervosa. Anorexia nervosa can profoundly damage/affect health and quality of life, and if left untreated can lead to severe and dangerous complications.

However, the level of your involvement will depend on the developmental age of your child. We use the term "developmental age" purposely. Everybody matures at a different rate, and to complicate matters even further, anorexia nervosa interferes with this maturing process. Your 18-year-old daughter may have a developmental age of 13 or conversely your 15-year-old may resemble a 20-year-old. What gets very confusing is that physical, emotional, intellectual and social development can each have different rates of maturation. There are no clear guidelines or rules but you have to be prepared to experiment and re-evaluate your opinion and attitudes in the light of events and accept that you will at times make mistakes

If you have read the first section and suspect your child has an eating disorder, try to discuss your worries with your partner or a friend. Ask them to read the section and then describe to them the symptoms you have noticed. If you believe there is a problem, plan a strategy together. If one of you thinks there is a problem and the other is uncertain or is unconvinced, meet in a week's time. Plan the next meeting carefully. Both of you should have time to report back and comment on your observations over the previous week.

These are some of the early signs that may indicate that your child is suffering from an eating disorder:

1.   You will notice your daughter is losing weight. She may disguise her new shape by wearing large baggy clothes.

2.   Your daughter may find ways of avoiding having meals with the rest of the family. She may say mealtimes don't fit with her timetable or that she is vegetarian and will prepare her own food. She may tell you she has already eaten or will eat later with friends. She may cook for the family but not eat herself.

3.   If your daughter does eat with the family you may notice her plate is piled high with vegetables and fruits to the virtual exclusion of food containing carbohydrates and fats. She may eat her food extremely slowly cutting it up into tiny pieces and pushing it around her plate.

4.   You may observe that she has become very active. She may have started going out for long walks or runs. She might have difficulty watching television with the family, instead becoming preoccupied with studying or exercising.

5.   Your daughter may start drinking a lot of coffee and diet cola drinks.

6.   You will see a change in her mood. She will become more tearful, irritable and impatient.

7.   She may have become withdrawn. She might have stopped going out with friends or participating in family events.

8.   She might binge eat. Large amounts of food will disappear from the fridge. You may find empty packets of biscuits and other foods in the bedroom.

9.   Your daughter may vomit. You may smell sickness or find vomit splashed around the bathroom.

10. You may come across empty packets of laxatives, or be aware that your daughter goes to chemist shops more often than before.

11. You may realise that your daughter is spending much longer in the bathroom. During meals or immediately afterwards she may go off to the bathroom. She may need to use the toilet several times at night.

AFTER RECOGNITION—WHAT NEXT?

Helping people to change their behaviour is not easy. Health psychologists who have a particular interest in helping people change their behaviour and lifestyle have identified five stages in this process.

1. Precontemplation: This first stage is when people are not even willing to think about their behaviour as a worry. They are therefore not motivated to do anything about it as they do not believe they have a problem.
2. Contemplation: In the next stage, people are willing to think that they have a problem. Sufferers are willing to examine the difficulties associated with their eating behaviour. Part of them may accept that their eating behaviour is a problem. They may be able to consider the implication of change. However, they take no constructive action. They may respond to confrontation or education but remain ambivalent and so do not take active steps.
3. Preparation: Sufferers may want to make changes and have a desire for help, but they are unsure what would happen if they gave up their eating behaviour. The factors that make it difficult to change still loom large.
4. Action: Individuals have made a commitment to change and started to modify their behaviour. They will have tried to modify the rigid control over their diet and begun to trust that they will be able to cope when they try something different. At this stage they will need a lot of support and encouragement.
5. Maintenance: Individuals continue the process and avoid relapse.

We have found that most people coming to our clinic are in the contemplation stage. They are willing to consider the idea that there might be something wrong but they are not sure about whether they can or want to change. As parents, you may find your daughter in the precontemplation stage.

People do not progress through these stages in an orderly manner and then improve. Some individuals go through the steps several times round and round, others get stuck at early phases. It is important to recognise the stage in a given individual. For example, if someone is in the precontemplation stage, they will not be ready for specific strategies for eating more. They may, however, be willing to discuss the problems they are confronting at this stage, such as feeling cold and lethargic. Many strategies can be used to help people move through the stages. All of them involve coming to some understanding about the reasons why change is so difficult. Angry confrontation does not get people to change but often serves to fix them more firmly in their own position.

Relatives and friends have an invaluable role to play in all stages. In the early stages of precontemplation/contemplation they can act as a resource and sounding board.

With the move into action, the role of family and friends is much less clear-cut as it depends on the young girl's development. For example, a developmentally young girl may need her family to steer her firmly into action. We will deal with this in more detail in Chapter 6. In this chapter we will focus on how you can address the problem and aid a move from precontemplation into contemplation.

ADDRESSING THE PROBLEM

It is best to plan clearly what you want to say to the affected person. Rehearsing, perhaps with a third party, can be helpful. Ideally, both parents should meet with their daughter. If you are a single parent you might ask your parents or siblings if they could help you. Plan a private and unhurried meeting. Aim to be direct but avoid arguing if at all possible as this may increase resistance. Calmly state what you have noticed that makes you suspect that she has an eating disorder. Give her a chance to respond. Ask her whether she has noticed anything herself that has concerned her. Do the symptoms you have noticed cause her any worry? Can she explain them? Ask if any of her friends or teachers have voiced concerns.

Ask her to consider some options to diminish your worries. Try to offer her a choice and give her time to think. Here is a list of ideas:

1. Read this book or another on anorexia nervosa and discuss it together afterwards.
2. Go to the general practitioner.
3. Go to the nurse at school or at the general practice and get weighed regularly.
4. Be weighed in a local shop and give the report to one parent.
5. Show by her actions that she is able to eat with the family and not find it difficult.

Plan to review the outcome of the options chosen in a week or two, when you need to have another planning meeting.

WHAT DO YOU DO WHEN YOU MEET WITH DENIAL?

When you confront your daughter with your worries that she has an eating disorder you may be met with defensiveness, denial or anger. The underlying reason for these reactions is that she is protecting herself and hiding her shame and fear—fear that you dislike her and fear that you will make her gain weight or eat. Be prepared for this type of response so that you do not get sucked into a row or retreat hurt.

If she becomes angry and shouts at you, acknowledge that although she has her own life, you also know that having an eating disorder clouds people's judgement. The more she denies that she has a problem the more she fits the characteristics of anorexia nervosa described in the first section. Stand firm. You have a right to be involved; because the eating disorder is affecting you and the family it is now also the family's business.

It is important that you remain calm during this session. Try to encourage her to describe her problems rather than bombarding her with your worries. For example, try to open up broad areas of discussion. You might ask her, "Have you any concerns about your health?" "Are there any particular worries you have?". Then ask "What about school? How are things going there? Are you concerned that you are not able to concentrate on your work as well as you used to?" "How are things with your friends? Are you finding it as easy to go out with them as usual?" "What about work? Have there been any difficulties there?" "What about here at home?" "Are there areas of concern?".

Once an area has been opened up, try to keep your foot in the door and explore it in detail. Think of yourself as an investigative journalist trying to get a detailed picture of the worry or problem.

It is often useful to show that you have understood the sufferer and to indicate that she has been listened to, by reflecting back what she has said. For example, "You have told me you have some concerns about your health. You have noticed that you are not sleeping as well as you once did. Your hair has become thin. Every time you wash it, handfuls seem to come out. I wonder whether this might have anything to do with your weight loss. What do you think about that?"

Here is an example of a possible scenario:

Father: Thank you for agreeing to come out for a walk with me. I thought it would be a good idea to get away from everyone else so that we wouldn't be interrupted.

Daughter: Hmm...............

Father: I do have something I am worried about and I'd like to talk to you about it.

Daughter: What?

Father: You have started to avoid family meals and you are losing weight rapidly.

Daughter: There's nothing wrong

Father: (Quietly) You don't think there is anything wrong? (Pause)

Daughter: No.

Father: Do you understand why I might be worried?

Daughter: No. There's nothing wrong. I am just a bit stressed at the moment.

Father: You are stressed at the moment?

Daughter: Yes.

Father: Does the stress you feel at the moment make it hard for you to eat?

Daughter: I suppose so.

Father: Let me make sure I have got it clear. You feel under stress at the moment and a consequence of that is that you are avoiding eating with the family. Is it interfering with your life outside of the family?

Daughter: Well I feel a bit cut off from everyone at school.

Father: You feel cut off from your school friends?

Daughter: Yes, I don't know why. I just don't seem to be able to join in any more.

Father: You don't seem to be able to join in with your school friends. Does that make it difficult to eat meals with them?

Daughter: Yes.

Father: Right, let me think. You have become stressed. You are not able to eat with us at home. You are not able to eat with your school friends and you feel isolated from them. Are there other things that are difficult for you at the moment? What about your health? I notice that you are wearing many more layers than you do usually. Is the cold getting to you more than usual?

Gradually, the daughter's rebellious stance softens as her father shows that he wants to listen and understand.

It is probably best to plan a staged approach with several meetings rather than to expect the problem to be ironed out when you first mention it.

It is often useful to sugar the difficult acknowledgement of a problem by indicating that treatment is possible, or to offer some sources of information or skills. Other self-treatment books are available (see reference lists). Also, books by fellow sufferers may be very helpful.

RESOLVING PROBLEMS

Once anorexia nervosa strikes communication within families becomes very difficult. As parents you may have become paralysed with fear and anxiety; you may be terrified about what may happen to your daughter; you may be distraught at the loss of her normal development and joy from life. Unfortunately this fear, worry, and sadness can make your interactions as a family become fraught. You will have tried insisting that your daughter eats. Unfortunately, head-to-head conflict of this kind does not work; it often makes the situation worse.

Imagine two objects accelerating towards each other with great force. What happens when they meet? There are three alternatives: (1) Object A could break; (2) Object B could break; or (3) A and B could be stuck together in deadlock. Parents and daughters with anorexia nervosa resemble this situation. Both of you are fuelled with great emotion which means that you are a force to be reckoned with, but you are coming from opposite directions. Collisions will only end in misery.

Let us go back to the two accelerating objects analogy. If you have one object accelerating off in one direction, a better way for the second object to influence the first, with both ending up intact and freely moving, is for the second object to run parallel with the first and gently to push from the side to make it veer towards a different path. This is the sort of approach that will be most successful when you are dealing with anorexia nervosa. It means that you will need to come at the problem from your daughter's perspective.

Anorexia nervosa is not stubbornness or naughtiness that can be stopped with a show of strength or power. It is an all-consuming irresistible force. Head-to-head conflict and confrontation will only end in tears or frustration. you will need to find ways of seeing things more from your daughter's point of view, with the hope that you can gradually shift the goals.

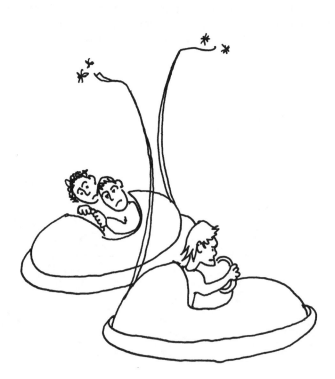

Research in psychology has proved that if you try to change behaviour which offers some benefit to the individual by confrontation, this will lead to rebellion and failure to comply. This is what happened with prohibition in the USA in the 1920s.

Successful and skilled negotiation in politics, business and interpersonal relations involves getting to understand the other person's point of view. What are their hopes and fears; what are the things that they hold dear; and what are the things that they would willingly sacrifice? Once you can understand the "opposition" agenda you may be able to find common ground.

How to do it

You need to find out more about your daughter's anorexia nervosa. What we are suggesting you do is not an easy task. It requires a lot of skill, training and practise. You will have to learn to sit on your hands, and not to try to solve things easily. It will not be easy for those of you who like action and problem-solving.

Start off by asking your daughter things like, "What are the good and the not-so-good things about the anorexia nervosa?". Once you have posed the question it will be important not only to *listen* (difficult task in many family interactions), but also to *understand* the replies. Understanding will not be easy because your daughter will be trying to describe confusing abstract concepts.

In order to make this as easy as possible you will need to attend to many things before you set up the listening time.

1. Ensure that you will be able to have a peaceful, quiet environment where you will be uninterrupted and where you will both be comfortable.

2. Sit near to each other but at a slight angle because, as an active listener, you will want to look at your daughter's face and body movements all the time, so that you can pick up the nonverbal cues she is displaying. A speaker is most comfortable if he or she can both look at and away from you.

3. Don't be afraid to leave a gap in the conversation while you pause and think about what has been said. Silences in this situation can be golden.

4. Make sure that you have understood what has been said. In order to do this try to paraphrase or repeat with different words what you thought you heard. This will give the opportunity for the speaker either to correct you or to carry on giving you more information.

5. If possible try to understand the emotion behind what is being said. Is there sadness, fear, or anger present? Name the emotion if there is one present. There is likely to be more than one present which makes it confusing.

6. The goal is to have a pattern of talking in which there is an even distribution of speaking.

7. At times try to summarise what you think you have heard and check out whether this is correct.

8. It is probable that your daughter feels it impossible to change because the positive benefits of staying anorexic and the negative aspects of trying to change far outweigh the perceived benefits of life without anorexia nervosa and any positive benefits of the change process.

9. Try to ensure that you can see both sides of this balance.

10. Gradually you may be able to think of alternative ways that the benefits of anorexia can be achieved by other means.

11. Alternatively, you may think of ways of making change more easy.

Steps 10 and 11 can only be undertaken if you have fully understood the present position. It may take several conversations before you reach this position.

An illustration of this sort of approach in a different context may help to make it clear.

John came home from school, slammed down his bag and uttered a string of expletives about his teacher, Mr Smith: "Mr S is a **** idiot."

John's mother was distressed to hear such language and challenged him: "John, I won't have you using that sort of language in my house. Mr Smith is a good teacher and you should show more respect."

John stormed off to his room banging the door.

If John's mother was using the negotiating rather than the confrontational approach she would have tried at first to understand her son's point of view. In this case she would have said something like: "It sounds as though you are upset and angry. What happened today?"

This would lead John to tell her more about what had happened. Once she had understood the whole situation, and John had felt understood and supported, she would then have been able to make a comment about language: "I understand how upset you must have felt about … I would prefer it if you wouldn't come in swearing as I find it unpleasant."

UNDERSTANDING WHY BREAKING OUT FROM ANOREXIA MAY BE DIFFICULT

Women with eating disorders have mixed feelings about getting better. There are many advantages to staying as they are whereas recovering and becoming "normal" may appear terrifying. Some of the reasons why patients with eating disorders are ambivalent about treatment are outlined in Table 5.1. Not all of these apply to every case and some are speculations rather than fact.

The social context

Anorexia nervosa can easily become a habit which is extremely difficult to shake off. In our society the affected person may be seen as rather special, someone who can diet and exert unusual self-control, or alternatively, someone who should be treated with kid gloves, shielded from demands, and from whom little should be expected.

TABLE 5.1   The positive reinforcers of anorexia nervosa

Context	State	Consequence
Social	Fashionably slim	Self-esteem is felt to rise
Family	Vulnerable yet powerful	Expectations lowered. Care increases, hostility decreases
Psychological	Control over food Empty stomach Overcoming physiology	Emotional distress alleviated Cleansed, therefore a better person Self-esteem felt to increase

The physical context

Some of the physical consequences of starvation may produce some benefits, especially in the short term. These are discussed in detail in Chapter 11. However, we will briefly mention some here.

The loss of menstruation and libido may be reassuring to those who have negative reactions to sexuality and menstruation. Although at first control over hunger is necessary, eventually appetite can be lost. This is thought to result from the production of ketones, a by-product of starvation and muscle breakdown. Stomach-emptying is delayed as a result of starvation, therefore eating leads to feelings of gastric fullness and physical discomfort. Overwhelming sensations of hunger re-emerge when weight gain begins. Therefore, any improvement in the pattern of eating can result in terrifying changes. People with anorexia nervosa may develop an aversion to food substances, particularly fats. It is as though they have conditioned themselves, or relearned, to perceive such food as unpleasant. One of our patients actually visualised the food inside her stomach. Muddy coloured mixtures of food particularly disgusted her. She could tolerate only foods that were white and "pure", such as cauliflower, cottage cheese and apples. Further examples of this are vividly portrayed in Jennifer Shute's book *Life size*.

The psychological context

These can be some of the most powerful reasons which prevent change. We have touched on some of them in earlier chapters. Anorexia nervosa often develops at a time of stress. It creates an illusion of coping as starvation can suppress emotional distress. Unfortunately, it is a strategy which avoids rather than solves problems. It is well known that if we try to avoid things this: (a) takes up lots of energy, and (b) only delays the time when we have to face the issues which do not go away. Worse than that, further difficulties are set in train and so the process continues. Some researchers have likened this process to an addiction. Indeed, sufferers talk of the "high" they get from starvation and from feeling in control.

IS THERE LIFE AFTER ANOREXIA?

Anorexia nervosa often arises at a time of great transition, and so it may be difficult to envisage life without it. What will "normal" life be like? Many sufferers have lost out on normal adolescence, a critical time for refocusing from family to peers, experimenting with an independent identity, developing life goals. One of the hardest aspects of the illness is that it is easy to lose touch with friends, the normal source of support in this period of change. Anyone who is the slightest bit timid will prefer to stay anorexic—"Better the devil you know than the one you don't know". One task on the way to recovery is to set reasonable goals which lead on to an appropriate change in lifestyle.

MOVING FORWARD ONCE THE SUFFERER ACCEPTS SHE HAS A PROBLEM

Remember that your daughter's developmental stage will determine how involved you are in this stage. If she is more mature she can begin to work on Section 3. And she might invite you to help with this.

However, for the less mature, these ideas may appear as rather abstract concepts and your daughter may need you to steer her clearly towards the path of recovery. It may help if you conceptualise the anorexia as a "minx" that has to be overcome.

Whatever ways you choose to help, it is important to have clear goals in mind and for these to be discussed with your daughter. Realistic goals will vary from sufferer to sufferer. Although full recovery may be an appropriate aim for younger sufferers with a short history of anorexia nervosa, it may not be realistic if, say, the illness has persisted for 10 years or more.

One of the most common pitfalls in dealing with anorexia nervosa is disagreement among those who might have some authority as to the way forward. In psychiatric circles this is called "splitting", in management terminology, "divide and rule". Ensure that you and others (general practitioner, psychiatrist, counsellor) involved are in broad agreement about your aims and approaches. Undermining can occur, if, for example, one person takes a tough line and the other a "softly, softly" approach. Or, if the individual who sets the limits is often away from home and unable to ensure that they are kept. Try to anticipate these difficulties and talk them out beforehand.

FURTHER READING

Shute, J. (1992). *Life size*. London: Secker & Warburg.

CHAPTER SIX

Pulling together as a family

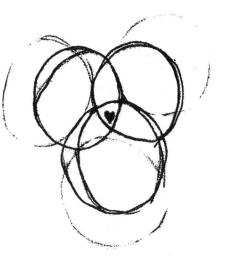

Families pass through various stages and it is impossible to write a chapter which will suit every case. Nevertheless, there are certain ground rules that apply to almost every case. You will need to use your judgement to decide what is appropriate for your family.

Being the parent of someone with anorexia nervosa is difficult. The illness disrupts family life. It is crucial that you continue to have your own life and don't neglect your spouse or other children. Make sure you set aside time to spend with them and on pursuing your own interests. You may find meeting the parents of other sufferers helpful. The Eating Disorders Association (see p.9 for the address) has lists of the network of parent's groups. The support of your friends and relatives can be invaluable.

Remember that you are a parent rather than a best friend to your anorexic child. Sufferers from anorexia nervosa are often caring, sensitive people and it can be tempting to unburden yourself to them. You may look to your daughter for support as another woman if the men in your life cause problems. Conflict can follow the resulting divided loyalties and abuse of trust. If your daughter has become your main confidante, try to make links with women friends. Don't be surprised or hurt if your daughter does not want to discuss all the details of her life or treatment with you; it is normal and healthy for adolescents to have secrets from their parents and this is part of the process of normal separation.

Many marriages are under strain in our Western society. Old values and expectations have been questioned. Over one-third of marriages end in divorce. Many people, however, struggle with difficulties within their marriage to find a solution. Although we do not think that difficulties within marriage cause eating disorders, they make coping with an eating disorder much more difficult.

As a parent it is important to provide your children with a framework of rules for living. They may fight against the rules but this is appropriate. Adolescents need rules to rebel against. Your child will feel more secure if you are able to take a firm stand on what you believe. Try to make sure that you know what you believe and the reasons underlying this belief so that when it comes to negotiation you know how far you will bend. If you have a partner, make sure the two of you present a united front to your anorexic child. Avoid being drawn into making decisions when you know your partner will disapprove. Remember that it is very important to avoid splitting (discussed in Chapter 5).

Have regular meetings outside mealtimes to decide the rules. Many families of adolescents, particularly those in which everyone is very busy, find it useful to set aside at least half an hour a week where they all sit together to discuss family issues. These will vary, they may be used to set ground rules, ask for help, review the week's events and/or plan future meals. You may find it useful to develop a checklist of rules for family life. Although no two families are the same and there are many different ways of living together successfully, certain rules are helpful to adopt when a family member is suffering from anorexia nervosa.

BASIC RULES

1. All members should respect each other. The parents should respect the child's move towards independence. The children should respect the need of their parents to spend part of their lives separately from the children. Each parent should respect the need of the other to lead part of his or her life independently.
2. Each family needs to decide what behaviour they find unacceptable and set limits on it. Specifically, parents as adults will place limits on their children's behaviour.
3. As parents you need to ensure that you are co-operating and enhancing rather than hindering each other's efforts.
4. Ensure that as parents you share the responsibility for your daughter equally (even if one takes the lead the other needs to support in other ways to maintain the balance of care).

5. As much as is possible with a debilitating illness such as anorexia nervosa, ensure that your daughter is moving towards becoming independent.
6. Make sure you have some time away from caring so that you can enjoy each other's company.

The following case examples illustrate what can happen when these basic rules get forgotten. Perhaps they remind you of what happens in your household.

Jennifer

Jennifer had suffered from anorexia nervosa since the age of 13. She had been in hospital five times. Jennifer was proud but also rather afraid of her father who was a successful businessman. She was concerned that she would not meet his standards. He was distressed and puzzled by Jennifer's problem. Her illness was one area of his life he couldn't control. He was often away on business leaving his wife with the day-to-day management of Jennifer. Jennifer's mother was exhausted and would be weeping when her husband telephoned home each evening. When he was at home he tried to help Jennifer eat. His wife had screamed at him, "Why don't you do something for a change?". He sat patiently while Jennifer shredded a slice of cucumber into 50 pieces and slid her hard boiled egg around the plate. After two hours he lost his temper and started to shout at Jennifer. In his anger he slapped her. He had never before hit her. Both Jennifer and her father were shocked. Jennifer's father left the house to calm down. His wife's response was sarcastic. "How can you do this to our daughter who is ill? She's not one of your employees." After this he stopped trying to help. Jennifer's mother oscillated between trying hard to be friendly and sympathetic, and becoming distant and sulky when she felt overwhelmed and hopeless. This impasse lasted over one more year and there were two more admissions.

Much patience and forbearance were needed for the family to work together. Jennifer's father arranged to arrive at work late each Monday morning so he and his wife could have a set time to discuss progress. They agreed on a joint plan that they both could handle. Jennifer's mother was able to steer a middle course and did not get hurt if Jennifer failed to finish her meal but noted it on the agenda the next week. Similarly, when Jennifer's father supervised a meal, he didn't feel it was a point of honour to ensure that he had won. At the Monday meetings both parents exchanged observations about what had seemed helpful and planned to test alternative approaches the following week. The parents were able to laugh together at mistakes they felt they had made and warmly responded when one of them was dispirited. The snipes and sneers of the previous two years vanished. Jennifer responded to this lighter atmosphere by gaining weight.

In other families long-standing difficulties may make it extremely difficult for the parents to work together. The following are examples of this.

Vanessa

Vanessa developed anorexia nervosa when she was 13. She lost weight quickly and was admitted to an adolescent unit. The parents indicated that they had difficulty working together. In an individual session Vanessa's mother, Hilary, told the therapist about their marital problems. She described a turning point in their marriage when her husband, Bill, hit her during an argument. She was outraged by this and, determined not to remain a victim, made plans to become financially more secure by working. She took up a teaching job when Vanessa was aged 7. The family moved into a new big house and both incomes were necessary to pay the mortgage. She was earning more than Bill but still had to negotiate with Bill over purchases. This led to frequent rows and, on a few occasions when he had been drinking, he hit her. They had had a particularly bad patch and had thought of separating before Vanessa's eating disorder began. Their marital difficulties were put on hold while they tried to work together to help Vanessa. These efforts were fraught with problems. Hilary was frightened of delegating to Bill as she feared that he would hit Vanessa. She said nothing about this fear but tried to shield Vanessa from Bill's anger. With parents so split, Vanessa's anorexia flourished.

Carla

Carla developed anorexia nervosa when she was 15. Her older brother, who was seven years her senior, had left home after finishing university. Carla was very close to her mother, Jenny, who used to complain to her about her husband, David. David was always out, whether working or in the pub after hours with his friends. Jenny and David had difficulty communicating. Jenny would talk and try to engage David in chatter but he would remain silent. Carla was Jenny's sounding board. It was impossible for Carla to understand the world of adult relationships as she was in many ways a child. Jenny never talked about the good things she got from her marriage. Carla, therefore, got a very one-sided picture, which fuelled her tendency to think in black and white terms. She thought mum should divorce dad. She got frustrated by her mother's obvious ambivalence. She therefore took matters into her own hands and started to behave as she thought her mother should. Carla refused to talk to dad and "divorced" him herself. Carla decided to leave home as she did not want to be supported by her father. It was as if she considered her mother to be almost prostituting herself by staying in the marriage. As Carla refused to talk to dad or even be in the same room, it was impossible to get the parents to work together to help Carla.

In the marriages described in these examples, the (basic) rules have been broken. In each of these families the first (i.e. that partners should respect each other) is broken. Jennifer's parents had adopted diverse roles but showed a tendency to undervalue each other. In Bill and Hilary's marriage there was overt sexism. Bill had difficulty adjusting to the new assertiveness and expectations of women. He expected to be able to exert his dominance over the family by physical and financial means. Jenny did not respect her husband's privacy when she talked to Carla about him, and behaved inappropriately when she used Carla as a sounding board for her difficulties. David and Jenny needed to try to communicate with each other.

IMPROVING COMMUNICATION

One thing we have stressed in several places in this book is the need to communicate with your daughter. This may seem an obvious point, but often rules of social interaction are ignored at home.

Communication is more effective if:

1. Only one person speaks at a time.
2. A person is talked to rather than talked about.
3. Speaking time is divided evenly.
4. Members understand what each other is saying.
5. Positive feelings are expressed.

Rules 4 and 5 need a little more explanation because they are less obvious and yet cause great difficulties. It can be all too easy to misunderstand what each other is saying. This happens because we all have our own assumptions or automatic reactions which are not necessarily shared with others. In a recent very popular book, *You just don't understand,* Tannen highlights the differences in communication styles between men and women and how this leads to friction. One way to ensure that this is not happening is to check that you have understood. You can do this by paraphrasing, to check that the meaning is understood or even repeating what was said. This can signal to the other person that they have been heard. So often in families, each member carries on speaking about his or her own agenda without evidence that they are considering the views of others.

All families have difficulties expressing positive sentiments to each other. We are all at our most grumpy and impolite at home. It has been noted that positive comments occur one out of ten, whereas the frequency of negative comments is nine out of ten. When families are under stress they make more negative statements. Try to find some positive things to note and make sure your comments are heard clearly:

- look at the person you are speaking to and speak in a warm tone,
- tell them exactly what they did to please you,
- let them know how it made you feel.

For example: "I am pleased that you were able to eat your meal with us tonight. It makes me feel that we are moving forward."

Similarly, if you want to request a change in behaviour, do so positively. Follow similar steps:

- tell the person how you would expect to feel if they perform that behaviour,
- look at the individual and speak in a firm but friendly tone,
- describe exactly what you would like the other person to do.

Examples of openers are: "I'd like you to ..." "I'd be most grateful if you would ..." "I'd be pleased if you ... ".

Negative expressions

Although bottling up negative thoughts is pointless and harmful, commenting on the negative like a dripping tap rarely produces a change in behaviour. It is best to delay expressing negative comments until they can be said calmly and clearly. Follow the same rules as for positive communication:

- look at the person you are talking to,
- describe clearly the behaviour that upset you,
- let them know how it made you feel.

For example: "Sally I felt upset and cut off when you ran out of the room last night and then refused to talk. Can we talk now so we can both understand what was going on?".

Play it cool: Cut the criticism

Illnesses and difficulties cause us all to get upset. Anorexia nervosa can be one of the most frustrating illnesses. The cure appears to simple: eating. And yet putting it into practice can be, oh, so hard! Also, recovery is slow. Getting over anorexia nervosa is not like getting over flu. Seeing how anorexia nervosa is destroying their daughter's life makes parents feel terrified and miserable. This mixture of anger, fear, despair and frustration can easily boil over and worsen the situation. Another vicious circle! Does the following scenario ring any bells?

Susan

> Susan had gradually been overcoming her eating disorder. She had joined in eating meals with the family. One day she was eating quiche and salad with her parents. Her mother suddenly asked, "When are you going to stop having a nervous breakdown over eating a piece of cheese?".

> Susan's mother was obviously feeling anxious and the remark slipped out. Unfortunately, this sort of critical comment can only increase the trouble. The easiest thing for Susan to do would be to flounce out of the room and skip her meal. In this case she didn't but it is important that you ensure that this escalating cycle doesn't start. Avoid criticism as much as possible as it leads only to revenge or despair. If there are behaviours you don't like, try to broach these with your daughter in a matter-of-fact way. Describe the behaviour you are unhappy about, taking care that your words do not appear attacking or insulting. The confrontation may be easier if you level your complaints at the anorexic "minx" part and try to collaborate with the "normal" part of your daughter.

Don't drown in despair

As a family you have to come to terms with feelings of loss when your daughter has anorexia nervosa. You will have lost the daughter you once had. A common complaint is that before the anorexia nervosa struck the daughter was as good as gold, perfect in many ways, but after the illness she became rebellious, stubborn and difficult to cope with. You may also have to deal with the loss of your ambitions and expectations. Often, both career and steps towards independence are interrupted. Sometimes these losses can hit the family so badly that overt depression occurs. Your daughter may become depressed because of the effects of starvation and the narrowed life that results from anorexia nervosa. You, as parents, may become depressed because the burden of caring for someone with anorexia nervosa is so great.

Hold your head up high: Shake off shame

Another aspect of the illness is the stigma attached. Even in the most forward-looking of communities, psychological illness carries a stigma. Anorexia nervosa is highly visible. Any passing person will notice your daughter's skeletal appearance. It is easy to feel guilty and ashamed and that you are to blame. Read on to the next chapter and realise you are innocent. The more you can share your problem with others the more likely you are to come up with creative ideas about how to help. It is no use trying to be an ostrich as the problem is plain to see. Some people, however, are reluctant to accept help, they fear that if they have used mental health services it will go on their record and will be a blot for life. If you are becoming emotionally drained or frazzled take steps to ensure that you get help. You may need to go to your general practitioner to see how he or she can help. You may want to attend a relatives' group linked with the Eating Disorders Association.

LIMIT-SETTING

Limit-setting is necessary in all cases of anorexia nervosa. However, the difficulty is that the illness usually occurs during adolescence when there would normally be a gradual stretching and changing of limits to fit with your child's maturation. Parents of daughters with anorexia nervosa may be given conflicting advice which adds to the family's difficulties. Sometimes you are told that you must take total charge of what your daughter eats. Others advise that there is nothing you can do to control your daughter's eating, that it is she who must decide what to do. If she hits rock bottom in the process, so be it. As a parent you might find yourself vacillating between no limits and unreasonable demands. The solution is to set limits that you believe in and are willing to defend if they are tested. We cannot tell you what these limits are. The exact boundaries of the limits are not so important as the fact that you as parents have agreed on them.

In specialised eating disorders units there are specified limits. For example, if we are working with a client as an outpatient, we will have a limit of undernutrition below which we will not work. If the patient continues to lose weight or fails to gain weight, we will ensure that they are admitted to hospital. In hospital, the limits are different. In a professional unit the limit will be weight gain of a fixed amount, for example, 1 kilo per week.

You need to spend a lot of time thinking out what limits to adopt and what action you will take if they are broken. The limits need to be capable of implementation. You will have to stand your ground despite persuasion, demands or threats.

PROBLEM-SOLVING

Families with a sufferer of anorexia nervosa have at least one problem: their daughter will not eat enough to maintain a normal weight. Commonly, there are other problems too. These may or may not relate to other aspects of the anorexia nervosa. If you as a family encounter a problem there are three basic strategies to deal with it:

1.   change the situation so you can overcome the problem,
2a.   adjust both desired and actual goals to a compromise position or;
2b.   alter your perception of the situation so it is no longer a problem,
3.   readjust goals so they are consistent with the present.

For example, with anorexia nervosa in the family, you can decide if you want to work towards your daughter regaining health. However, if your daughter has been ill for 30 years despite many attempts at treatment, you may decide to accept that your daughter will remain disabled by her illness but you will do all you can to help her make her life as comfortable and safe as possible. Or you might work towards a compromise solution in which you help your daughter maintain her weight above the crisis level but you don't nag her with expectations of grandchildren or even a job. The following is an example of how one family learned to cope better with their daughter's anorexia nervosa.

Julia

Julia, aged 24, developed anorexia nervosa when she was away at university. Her tutors would not let her continue her course. She came back home to live. Julia's parents were very worried and did all they could to help. However, if they tried to help with a meal, Julia became rebellious, would walk off and not eat anything. Julia's mother took all the setbacks and fluctuations in Julia's eating and weight personally. Her worrying brought on migraines. Her husband would then be doubly irritated to find his wife ill in bed in a darkened room and to have to face his daughter's continuing anorexia. The parents discussed this problem together.

They decided that unlike many other problems that they had faced in their family life, this was one they couldn't solve practically. They decided that, as their daughter was attending a specialist clinic, they would try not to be so involved in the minutiae of the anorexia. They understood from the specialist that Julia's anorexia could take five or more years to burn out or be worked through. They therefore were able to take a longer-term view of the illness and did not expect too much too soon.

Problems are a fact of life and we have to accept them and how they affect us. A perfect solution may not be available but there are often effective alternatives. Patience helps in detecting the best way forward.

Understanding the problem. If you have a problem it needs to be clearly defined. All the facts and information about the problem should be gleaned. Take a Sherlock Holmes approach: who, what, when, where, why and how? The facts need to be described with detachment as though they are to be presented on a news bulletin. It is necessary to be as specific as possible. What elements of the situation make it a problem? Sometimes assumptions or premature judgements turn an event into a problem. Get everyone's views on the difficulty, especially your daughter's.

Generating solutions. Once the problem is defined you need to think of as many solutions as possible. Keep a written list so that you do not forget any. If you come up with any really wacky ideas, write them down as sometimes these contain a germ of truth or can spark off many new ideas. It is important that this brainstorming phase takes place as creatively as possible. Do not prematurely criticise any of the solutions. This is a hard task for families with a member suffering from anorexia nervosa, as high standards often abound. It is important to remember that the goal of this stage is to produce as many, practical or impractical, solutions as possible. Put your critical hat on later. You want quantity not quality.

Choosing a solution. Once you have a list of solutions the next stage is to choose the best option. It may be helpful to write down the pros and cons of each one. You may need to compromise or plan to try one out with the proviso that you will later go on to another if it fails. Once you have decided on your solution make sure the family agrees about how it will be implemented. What is the first step? Does anyone see any blocks which will prevent this taking place? Make sure it is clear who is to do what. Write it down if possible so that you all can agree on what has been said.

Review.   Set aside time to review progress. Were any of the steps involved in finding the solution too difficult to carry out? Are further skills or resources needed? Is it a good idea to go back and choose a different solution or does it make more sense to find ways round this roadblock? If the solution has worked, sit back and make sure you congratulate yourselves. Go out and give yourselves a family treat.

Here is how Charlotte and her family tackled their problem:

Charlotte

Charlotte was 16. She had been vegetarian for four years. At 15, she had had an operation on her hip. Complications occurred and she eventually had three operations. She was in hospital for several months. Her weight gradually fell over this period. Charlotte was delighted, as she considered herself and her family rather plump. She had been teased since she was 11, just prior to puberty when she had had some puppy fat. Two months before her parents brought her to the clinic she became vegan and her weight continued to fall. Her parents were concerned as she had lost 2 stone, had not had a period for 9 months and was preoccupied by counting calories and reading cookery books. Charlotte did not agree that she had a problem, and was firm in her resolve not to gain too much weight. "I've done my time as a fat person", she said. Her parents decided they wanted to tackle her diet. They sat down with Charlotte and produced the following ideas:

1. Force Charlotte to give up a vegan diet and make her eat what the rest of the family were eating.
2. Put the whole family on a vegan diet and make Charlotte eat with them
3. Come to a compromise and ask her to return to being vegetarian until her growth and development had finished and she had given the operations on her hip time to heal. (After such an operation bone remodelling might take up to one to two years.)
4. Go with her to a specialist dietician with expertise in vegan diets.
5. Let Charlotte stay on a vegan diet but ensure that she had protein, oil and mineral supplements.

Once they had drawn up this list of alternatives the family considered the pros and cons of each option. They decided to go for option 4. Father was given the job of implementing this. He contacted the dietician's professional organisation for a list of names. Charlotte and her family decided to judge the usefulness of this step by monitoring Charlotte's weight. They agreed that her weight should increase by half a kilo each week. If no progress was made in six weeks they would consider changing to one of the other options.

After the visit to the dietician Charlotte added 115–170g of nuts into her diet each day. She slowly increased her weight so that it was in the normal range. After six months her periods had returned.

IS IT YOUR SPOUSE WHO HAS ANOREXIA NERVOSA?

Although many of the things we have described apply just as well if it is your spouse who has anorexia; there are some differences.

You most probably will have found that your partner's illness has affected your life in many ways. Like anyone who lives with a sufferer you need to look after your own well-being. If you have children, you may need to give them extra attention as your partner may be too ill to look after them as she might wish.

Here are some basic aims that you may want to try to keep in mind:

1.   Maintain a balance of power between you. (It's easy to give in to the demands of the illness.)
2.   Aim to increase or focus on the aspects of the relationship which give you pleasure.
3.   Ensure that you both have time off. Let your spouse have time off from care-giving.

The sexual side of your relationship will probably have suffered. It is important not to assume that a sexual relationship will resume immediately on weight gain. It often takes time. You may need to rebuild your relationship by doing the things you enjoyed when you first met. After a long period of illness, we often find that both partners may need some help rebuilding their sexual life.

FURTHER READING

Asen, E. (1995). *Family therapy for everyone. How to get the best out of living together*. London: BBC Books.

Skynner, R., & Cleese, J. (1989). *Families and how to survive them*. London: Mandarin.

Tannen, D. (1992). *You just don't understand: Women and men in conversation*. London: Virago.

CHAPTER SEVEN

What can be done about eating?

We mentioned earlier that it is difficult for anyone to prescribe what families should do to help because it all depends on the developmental age of the child.

The family of an adult sufferer can help by giving the information, resources and feedback that facilitate the move from the stages of precontemplation to contemplation and preparation. During the action phase family members will probably be needed to give care, support and advice, and to act as an emotional buffer.

However, with younger sufferers the complex abstract psychological processing and understanding needed to move into action is developmentally too sophisticated. Parents therefore have to step in and guide their child into action. There are no strict chronological cut off points, each set of parents need to make their own decision. Of course, this may also apply to some adults if they have lost insight into the severity of the illness.

STAGES OF TREATMENT

Treatment of anorexia nervosa usually has three parts: the first is restoration of a healthy weight or some weight gain to prevent dangerous physical problems, the second is helping the sufferer combat her anorexic attitudes, and the third is understanding the personality features and difficulties which may have increased the risk of developing an eating problem. Treatment does not necessarily take place in this sequence. It is important to start treatment early in the course of the illness because, once it sets in, many other problems emerge.

Families who have a young child with anorexia nervosa will need to be more actively involved in overcoming the anorexic behaviour. For example parents may need to supervise meals and prevent compulsions taking control. It is hard work but it has compensations. One of the advantages is that links with friends, school, etc., are easier to maintain. On the other hand, an advantage of inpatient treatment is that in specialist units, other sufferers can give help and support. This means that problems can be shared, reducing isolation and alienation. It may be possible to recreate this at home by joining the Eating Disorders Association (see p.9) who run local self-help groups.

Remember that 12–14 full-time nurses are required to staff an eating disorders unit. At home you are lucky if one of you is able to devote a significant amount of time to the problem. It's therefore not surprising if you find helping exhausting. Beware of "burn out". Make sure you are able to recharge your batteries. *One difficulty for parents is they cannot treat their daughter with clinical detachment.* Often the level of empathy is so great that it is difficult to distinguish between the anorexic "minx" and the normal non-anorexic part of your daughter. Try to become as well informed about the illness as you can. Read as many books as possible. This will help you to know what is anorexia talking and what is reasonable.

FIRST THINGS FIRST

As low weight has an adverse effect on the mind it is not possible to tackle anorexic attitudes without also tackling life-threatening starvation. It is unhelpful to spend a lot of time speculating about hidden, underlying reasons as to why the anorexia developed: the illness may only gain an increasingly tighter stranglehold. In Chapter 11 we discuss how many of the consequences of starvation are self-perpetuating. A primary task, therefore, of a parent or partner of someone suffering from an eating disorder, is to work with the sufferer to find a way of preventing further weight loss.

What do I do about food?

Again this depends in part on the sufferer. She may have reached the stage where she is trying hard to get well and has asked for your help. Alternatively, as a responsible parent you may need to step in to stop your daughter compromising her health or social and career development or even putting her life at risk. Do not be frightened of doing this even if you fear that your daughter is too old for you to adopt this role. Remember that insight into the dangers and risks of anorexia nervosa is lost once the condition really takes a hold.

Never let her talk you into going on a diet. Don't buy slimming magazines or low calorie foods for her or the rest of the family. Stick to a healthy diet of normal foods. Trying to tempt her to eat with special meals of all her favourite foods is a trap that is easy to fall into. Despite your efforts, your daughter will probably refuse to eat, leaving you feeling rejected after all your hard work. Similarly, filling the fridge with "naughty" tempting foods is not helpful. If she succumbs she will only feel more mortified than ever.

The journey towards a normal, healthy diet is best taken a step at a time. For the sufferer, reducing her over-controlled behaviour and facing the consequences of weight gain is extremely difficult. It may be useful to follow a carefully calculated, individual plan to produce a predictable, steady gain (see end of this chapter). A dietician can help with this. Taking the person through the calculations to estimate her individual energy needs can help build her confidence that her weight can behave predictably. Use of standard equations (e.g. WHO, 1985) produces a reasonably accurate estimate of how many calories a day need to be eaten to maintain a healthy weight.

To increase the sufferer's variety of food, it is more realistic for you to help her make a series of small changes rather than attempt an immediate move to "normal". Small snacks will probably be easier for her to eat than normal-sized meals. The feeling of a bloated, distended stomach is less marked, and the food itself seems less daunting in limited quantities. She will most likely be able to eat larger amounts of "safe" foods, while moving more gently toward increased amounts of "risky" foods. For example, a first step towards fattier foods may be low fat spread, semi-skimmed milk, or tuna fish. A first move towards more sugary food may be a muesli bar, or fruit yogurt. For someone who has never eaten breakfast, a glass of orange juice can be a start with toast added later, then maybe cereal. It is *always* necessary to eat enough to prevent weight loss, and to promote weight gain if necessary. But normal eating does not have to resume immediately.

Mealtimes—If your daughter lives at home with you

Your daughter may have become very interested in food and want to do the cooking for the family. This is not the good sign it may seem. Explain to her that while she is ill you will not let her cook for the family, as this is part of her anorexic preoccupation with food. You may decide that she can cook meals for herself but that if she fails to gain weight you will cook for her. Try to have regular family mealtimes. Let her know that you would like her to try to eat with you, but don't be surprised if she doesn't or only manages a very little. Try your very hardest not to make mealtimes the focus of family conflict. Food is already a terrifying issue for her and fighting about it will only make it more so.

PROBLEMS

A common occurrence is for feelings of hunger to reappear with a vengeance once a pattern of eating re-emerges. This is very frightening for the sufferer—her worst nightmare come true. She fears that she will become bulimic, that she will never be able to stop eating and will blow up like a balloon. This is a normal phase. It does not mean that individuals will get bulimia nervosa. Men who were starved as part of an experiment in the 1950s went through a phase of binge eating when they were allowed access to more food. Victims of famine binge eat when food arrives. Out-of-control overeating develops as a result of weight loss and, of course, in anorexia nervosa, by definition, weight loss is large. If the so-called binges are analysed they are often not that big and the daily intake including the contents of the binge is often well below the recommended calorie level.

We can understand why this pattern develops as it represents one of the body's feedback control mechanisms. Only recently have scientists been able to fully understand how the composition of the body (the ratio of lean to fat etc.) is controlled. They have been able to use genetic biology and have found that some strains of rats are obese because they lack the gene which controls the formation of a "satiety" protein produced by fat cells. The body acts as if it has a lipostat, that is, a monitor which can detect how much fat tissue there is in the body. Fat tissue secretes a protein which acts on the brain to control appetite and metabolism. If the amount of fat tissue is low, little of this "satiety" protein is produced. This leads to increased appetite. Conversely, once the fat tissue reaches normal levels higher amounts of this "satiety" protein are secreted and appetite falls.

The amount of this "satiety" protein produced therefore depends on the genetic make-up and on the state of nutrition (i.e. the size of fat stores). This breakthrough in understanding how body composition was controlled only occurred in 1994 and there are still many questions left unanswered. One of these is how does anorexia nervosa override this feedback mechanism? Does this mechanism swing into normal action as soon as the sufferer begins to eat or is it still impaired?

We are certain of some facts. People at risk of anorexia nervosa do not appear to have the obesity gene, that is, they are able to produce normal levels of the "satiety" protein. Commonly, the families of sufferers with anorexia nervosa tend towards leanness rather than obesity. Body composition returns to normal after recovery from anorexia nervosa. Anorexia nervosa does not lead to obesity.

Therefore, the increased hunger that occurs during weight recovery is a temporary and normal phase. It will gradually pass if small regular meals are eaten throughout the day. Bulimia need not become a habit. It is only the abnormal pattern of eating and the weight control measures that lead to the spiral of symptoms that make up bulimia nervosa. (For more details about how to manage bulimia nervosa we suggest you read Schmidt & Treasure's *Getting better bit(e) by bit(e)*. For example, it is important to eat regular meals throughout the day. This prevents severe hunger developing. Eating carbohydrates, especially starchy foods such as potatoes, frequently maintains a high blood sugar level, and so prevents hunger. Short intervals between episodes of eating are easier to cope with for someone who is obsessed by food, as it is easier to find a distracting activity to fill an hour or two. Keeping a record of eating and drinking can help the sufferer to feel more objective and rational about her eating behaviour. Her anxiety reduces and, in time, she has a record of progress to build her confidence and confirm that her efforts are effective.

ACTIVE INVOLVEMENT IN EATING

This level of involvement will depend on the development stage of the sufferer and also whether the level of starvation is so severe that the capacity for rational thought is lost. There are many ways of ensuring that your daughter has a regular eating pattern. In some families one or both parents sit with their daughter during her meal. It may be necessary to encourage her when eating becomes difficult. This may take the form of talking her through every mouthful. For example, "That's right, now take another forkful, in it goes. Now another". If this degree of supervision is needed, one-to-one interaction may be called for. If your daughter takes a very long time to eat, you may have to set aside an hour to sit with her during the meal. Plan an enjoyable event afterwards, such as a walk together, if she finishes in the allotted time. Whatever plan(s) you adopt it is important to have regular meetings to review progress and plan further strategies.

One option is to use high calorie drinks from the chemist or from your general practitioner if eating become too slow or difficult.

This is how Clare's parents explained their use to her. They decided to adopt this approach after she had spent 3–4 hours on each meal: "I know how difficult it is for you to eat, but I am not going to stand by and see you destroy your life and your health. I want you to drink up these supplements as food is too difficult at the moment." Once you have set these limits it will be necessary to stick to them. Adopting this role will be uncomfortable, but reassure yourself that it is no different to giving your child unpleasant anticancer drugs that will make her feel sick and lose her hair in the short term but will give her life. In fact the position is easier than this because although there is some discomfort with refeeding, quite rapidly you will see your daughter's hair, skin and circulation improve.

As she gains weight, you may need to reassure her that the food will not make her fat but will be converted to healthy muscle and bone. Discussing the benefits of being a healthy weight again may also help. You may find yourself like a broken record repeating phrases such as: "You are not getting fat. You need to eat to solidify your bones." You may decide that talk about weight or shape should be banned but you will need to use constant reminders to enforce this: "I think that it is your anorexic part talking. We agreed that I would not converse with that part as it is destructive and illogical. Let's discuss issues which are of relevance to your normal part."

Isobel

Isobel started to lose weight when she was aged 11 following a change in school. Isobel's mother sat with her and encouraged her daughter to eat slowly. She found it was essential to keep talking in a gentle way. If she saw that her daughter was stopping she would say, "I know that it is difficult for you to eat, and that is the anorexic part, but it is important for you to eat so that the normal part recovers its health. Keep on eating to sustain the part of you that I want to grow and develop". Isobel and her mother used the opportunity to discuss the events of the day. Her mother used to recount tales of Isobel's life from the day she was born, events during her childhood and also talk about events from her own life. In this way the protracted mealtimes passed reasonably smoothly. Isobel's mother made sure that during this time she was not distracted by her other children or household tasks. She arranged for her mother to come in and feed the other children and supervise their homework, or on some days her husband would come and take the other children away. She put the telephone on to the answering machine.

Barbara's family adopted another approach.

Barbara

Barbara was 22 when she developed anorexia nervosa and had been living away from home. However, when Barbara's anorexia had been present for three years and was interfering with her career and social life she decided to return home so that she could get her parents' care and support. She preferred this option to going into hospital. She and her parents decided to let her be totally independent about her meals. She went to the shops and bought food for herself. She ate her food in the dining room alone. Her parents agreed that they would not enquire about her food intake other than to ask her whether she was making progress in terms of weight. She arranged to go to her general practitioner each week where she was weighed by the practice nurse. She let her parents know that she was making progress. Gradually, she was able to eat meals with the family.

It is often sensible to have some outside reference point to establish whether the work you are doing at home is progressing or whether a new solution needs to be decided. Being weighed regularly by a neutral party such as a practice nurse is often helpful.

Other families have come up with other solutions.

Jane

Jane and her parents found that mealtimes became highly tense and it was difficult to defuse the atmosphere. They came upon the solution that Jane would go each evening to her grandmother's and have her meal with her. Her grandmother had much more time and was able to be more relaxed and Jane felt it easier to eat in these surroundings.

WHAT IS THE CORRECT AMOUNT TO EAT?

In hospitals, because of the need to avoid prolonged inpatient treatment, the range of weight gain is set between 1 and 2 kilograms per week. At home it is not necessary to have such a large goal and this can be negotiated. See Chapter 12 for more exact calculations on calorie consumption. To gain a kilogram (2 pounds) in weight, an extra 7700kcal over and above the basal level needs to be eaten. What does this mean? The normal metabolic requirements are about 2000kcal a day, so if you want to gain a kilogram (2 pounds) a week you would have to eat 3000kcal a day. This means a normal amount of food plus half again. If the goal is to gain 0.5 kg (1.1 1bs a week), you would need to eat an extra 500 calories each day on top of the normal calorie requirement of 1500–2000. Therefore, it is necessary to eat between 2000–2500kcal per day to gain weight at this steady rate. It often comes as quite a surprise to realise how much needs to be eaten to gain weight.

The increased calorie consumption can be taken in the form of snacks, for example, a sandwich at 11am and 3pm and a banana before going to bed at night. In other families, food supplements such as Ensure, Complan or meal replacements are used. Ready-made meals and prepacked snacks can eliminate deliberations about what to give to your daughter.

WHAT SORT OF FOOD?

If the degree of starvation is severe, low roughage food is sensible. This is because muscle has been lost from the gut wall and it may be difficult for the gut to cope with too much bulk. Do not worry if the diet is repetitive. For example, a baked potato and cottage cheese three times a day is acceptable. It is best to stick to a routine and gradually introduce new foods, as too much novelty will cause the sufferer to feel guilty and fearful.

Do not be bullied or bamboozled. Many parents say, "Yes, but you should see the amount she eats, it's more than I do". Commonly, people with anorexia nervosa eat large amounts of low calorie foods, such as vegetables and salads. Do not have the wool pulled over your eyes. Insist that food of an adequate calorie density is eaten. Some high quality protein foods, such as fish, are necessary. Choose fish which decreases the risk of heart disease (e.g. sardines, mackerel, tuna and salmon). A good guide for foods with the correct balance for growth and recovery are seed foods (e.g. bananas, avocados, beans and nuts).

Don't get bullied into providing a fat-free diet. Some oils are essential. They are critical for cell growth. The health education message about fats has been written for overweight middle-aged men not for women with anorexia. Cholesterol levels are high in the starvation state of anorexia nervosa (see Chapter 11). They return to normal after weight gain. Point out this paradox if you are challenged with a "healthy eating" argument.

Here is an example of a diet plan. It is unlikely that this is a suitable first goal. You don't need an expert dietician to tell you what to feed your daughter. There is nothing subtle and complex about the dietary requirements. It is simple *adequate calories*, that is, a dietary intake of over 2000 calories per day.

Thelma's Diet Plan:

> *8.15am - Breakfast.*
> Fruit juice
> 1 small box cereal
> 200ml skimmed milk
> 1 slice brown bread
> 1 pat margarine/butter
> 1 spoon marmalade
> 1 pot tea or coffee
> *10.30am - Mid-morning*
> Coffee with milk (skimmed)
> 1 avocado or banana
> *12.30pm - Lunch*
> Main course - piece of grilled meat or prepared salad or vegetarian dish
> Pudding - yoghurt, fruit salad or fruit
> 1 cup of tea/coffee
> 1 cup of water
> *3.30pm - Mid-afternoon*
> Tea with skimmed milk
> Yogurt or 2 plain savoury biscuits or sandwich
> *6.30pm - Supper*
> Main course - same as lunch
> Fruit /yogurt
> 1 cup of water
> 1 cup of tea with skimmed milk
> *Bedtime*
> Hot drink with skimmed milk and banana

It may be easier if the sufferer follows exactly the same diet each day and gradually makes exchanges to increase her variety of foods. So fish could be switched for chicken and a pear for an apple.

Louise

Louise had lost weight rapidly and was a vegetarian. She had been eating fruit only for the weeks before she was seen. She came to the clinic dragging her foot because the nerves to her foot were not working properly. Also she could not get up from a crouching position.

> *Breakfast*
> Glass skimmed milk

2 oatcakes spread with smooth peanut butter
Apple
10.30am - Snack
Coffee made with skimmed milk
2 oatcakes spread with peanut butter
Banana
12.30pm - Lunch
Baked potato with cottage cheese
Fromage frais
3.30pm - Snack
Milky coffee or milkshake made with skimmed milk and
    frozen fruit
2 oatcakes spread with peanut butter
Supper
Baked potato with cottage cheese
Fromage frais
Snack
Milky drink
Banana

This diet is high in calcium which helps to restore nerve and muscle
function.

Susan

Susan found that if she went to her supermarket and bought
ready-made meals she felt secure in that she didn't have to weigh
her food. She was able to supplement two meals from this with
snacks, such as a peanut butter sandwich and a glass of milk which
she kept constant.
Here is her diet plan:

Breakfast
Milky coffee
2 Weetabix with milk
Snack
Crunch bar
Milky drink
Lunch
Prepared meal
Yoghurt
Snack
Pack of nuts and raisins

Milky drink
Supper
Prepared meal
Yogurt
Snack
Piece of fruit cake
Yoghurt drink

You can probably think of many other sorts of snacks. Your list might include a peanut butter sandwich, a packet of fruit and nuts, an avocado, a crunch bar, a bowl of cereal, etc.

ACTIVE INVOLVEMENT IN CHANGING
WEIGHT CONTROL MEASURES

Laxatives

It is important that you do not get involved in purging behaviour. *Never* buy laxatives for your daughter or give her the money to buy them for herself. If you do this, it suggests that you approve of what she is doing. Explain to her that using laxatives is part of her illness and is physically harmful. Tell her that as you care about her you cannot help her harm herself but that you are there for her and will help her to get better when she is ready.

Vomiting

If you suspect that your daughter is vomiting, don't pretend that it isn't happening; state your reasons factually but don't get too critical or disgusted. Let her know that you realise how upsetting this is for her and how guilty she may feel. Remember that emotional blackmail never helps, so don't try to make her feel guilty about upsetting you. Just point out the damage she is doing to herself. Offer to help her combat the urge to vomit, perhaps by quietly sitting holding hands after meals even if this takes two hours or more.

As a general rule, it is unhelpful for you as a parent to set rules for your daughter without her consent. You may encounter only deception and manipulation. The aim in your negotiations with your daughter is to listen to her concerns and ensure that she is aware of the reasons for your worries. For example, you need to explain that you are concerned because she is putting her life at risk and may cause herself long-term problems. Try to find a chink in your daughter's armour of indifference to the consequences so that you can work together. Set goals that are realistic. It is not appropriate to say: "You must not vomit again." This is too high a target and will lead to failure and relapse.

This is how the mother of Rosemary, a girl who was very underweight and also vomited frequently, voiced her anxiety:

> Your father and I are very concerned about your health. We know that you also recognise some difficulties. You have told me how, on occasions you feel extremely tired. Going out with your friends is now too much of an effort. I think these problems result from your anorexia and vomiting. We would like you to have a better quality of life. We would like to help. Here are some ideas we have: one possibility would be for me to stay with you for three hours after each meal. Another possibility would be for us to lock the bathroom door. Alternatively, you could promise us that you will delay your vomiting by at least an hour after each meal. Can we discuss this further together?

Exercise

Exercise may seem a healthy activity but it is used by some sufferers in an obsessive way to control their weight or felt as a drive that needs to be obeyed. It is imperative to suppress this overactivity when someone is at a very low weight. This is because the body's danger signals which indicate overwork often may not be noticed or are ignored in people with anorexia nervosa. In other cases, the drive to overexercise overrides the pain of stress fractures. Patients with anorexia nervosa are at risk of fractures as their bones are very thin. Other sufferers continue to exercise even though they develop friction-induced sores. As the skin is so dry and fragile in anorexia nervosa these take a long time to heal.

Patricia

> Patricia spent the whole day on the go. She would walk long distances, go swimming for two hours and do step aerobic classes. Her parents expressed the view that they were concerned that she was wearing out her body and that she needed more balance within her life. They therefore agreed to help her set realistic goals. She reduced by one hour each week the amount of time she was walking. She stopped swimming. She decided to continue the aerobics class on three nights per week because there was a social element which she valued.

What is an acceptable amount of exercise? When weight loss is severe no exercise at all is advisable. A reasonable amount of exercise is a half hour three times a week when your weight is out of the anorexic range; that is, above 17.5kg/m^2.

Many parents are exasperated by the thought that excessive exercise may rush to fill the place of dieting restriction. It may, but there are advantages in this route to perfection. Exercise is much more culturally acceptable and does not lead to such social isolation as anorexia nervosa. Also, it is not as damaging to health.

Jane

Jane had had anorexia nervosa for 12 years. She became critically ill and was admitted to hospital for tube feeding on several occasions. Her brother returned to live in her home town after he had been away at university. He suggested that if Jane could keep her weight up after her last admission she would be able to go to the gym with him. Jane became interested in step aerobics which she started doing twice a week. After three months, holding her weight steady, she began to train as a teacher. Two years later her periods had returned, she was at a normal weight and she gave lessons in step aerobics.

TAKING STOCK

You need to set aside time on a regular basis to review progress. Weight is the only yardstick to consider if your daughter is underweight and still losing. It may be possible to consider other goals if weight is stable and not life-threatening. Don't let yourself get sidetracked into lengthy discussions about uncertain markers of progress. If weight is not increasing, the solutions that you and she have come up with to gain weight have not been working. Use the tactic of joining with her against the anorexia minx. Don't let yourself get too emotionally roused as your ability to think of solutions will be impaired. Don't take failure personally.

Ask her if she knows why the solutions have not worked. Can she come up with some alternatives? Work with her to generate a variety of options which might need to be considered. Does she require more foods. What foods would she like to introduce? Does she want more help from anyone? Can you ask grandma to come and stay and devote herself to the problem? Do you or your husband need to consider taking time off work? Do you need to ask friends to help with other children? Do you need to consider hospital admission? By generating a variety of options you both feel that there is an element of choice. It may be necessary to come back to some of the options. So write them down as "minutes" of your meeting along with the final decision taken.

People with low self-esteem have a tendency to be over-sensitive to failure, and are unable to recognise success. When it is pointed out to them, people with an eating disorder will often recognise in themselves a tendency to perfectionism, to write off their efforts as failure unless they have been totally successful, which is, of course, impossible in many situations. It can help to have achievements pointed out, highlighting progress in treatment. A diary, building up a record over a period of time, may be helpful. Such a record may also encourage you as you see your daughter improving. As an individual's confidence increases she can gradually take over responsibility for feeding herself.

If your daughter is not at the stage where she wants/needs active help with eating ask her if there is other help she may need. Perhaps there are other things with which you can help her—see the next chapter.

FURTHER READING

Schmidt, U., & Treasure, J. (1993). *Getting better bit(e) by bit(e)*. Hove, UK: Psychology Press.

WHO (World Health Organisation) (1985). Diet nutrition and prevention of chronic diseases. *Technical Report Series 797*. Geneva: WHO.

CHAPTER EIGHT

More than mere fattening up

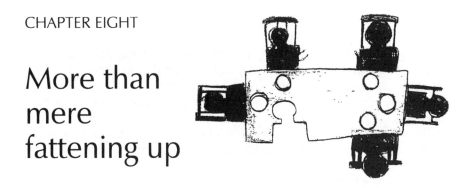

Sufferers from anorexia nervosa have confused views about their bodies. For example, if you comment on the weight gain and improved appearance of someone with anorexia nervosa, you will not reassure them—rather, you may alarm them.

APPEARANCE AND BODY IMAGE

Commonly, women with eating disorders talk about feeling fat even though they might on some level recognise that they are thin. This statement should perhaps be taken as an explanation of why eating is difficult: the sufferer feels as if she is fat and does not need or deserve food. You may need to confront your daughter with the reality of her thinness. Obtain a photograph of your daughter as she is at present. In a warm, supportive atmosphere look at this photo together and contrast it with a picture taken before the illness arose. Often, people with anorexia nervosa avoid any confrontation with reality. They do not look in mirrors. They find it difficult to see themselves as others see them. It may be helpful to stand with your daughter in front of a mirror and slowly and calmly look at the reflection.

Another strategy that you might want to try, is to say that you want to pretend that you are both in court. You will play the prosecutor and say that she is too fat and she must play the part of the defence lawyer, arguing that your client the Anorexia Minx (AN) is not fat—it would go something like this:

(*Prosecutor*) Members of the jury I contend that the accused Anorexia Minx is so fat that she was unable to enter through the doors of the court in the usual way, but she had to step in sideways.

(*AN as defence lawyer*) That is not true, she was able to enter the door normally.

(*Prosecutor*) Members of the jury, I declare that Anorexia Nervosa Minx is so fat that she was unable to sit in the court seat etc., ...

Aim to start with ridiculously exaggerated pictures and gradually come down to issues such as clothes size, etc.

Another approach is to get some size 16 clothes from a shop where you can try them on at home and return them. Size 16 is the average size of a British woman. Suggest that the sufferer tries on these clothes. Ask her what she makes of it? Is she bigger than average?

Other ways of confronting reality may be to question our present cultural stereotypes. Rosemary's mother took her to Hampton Court where they toured the house and looked at the portraits. Rosemary was interested to notice that all the women in the portraits were plump by today's standards. She was thus able to contemplate the possibility that modern standards were really reflections of fashion. It is helpful to study books which have questioned our present culture of thinness (see the reading list on page 132. It is not helpful to have too many fashion magazines around the house. (One of my patients called these magazines and those with recipes "anorexia porn"!) Research has shown that these can increase distress.

Dealing with social events

Social events can be very difficult for those with anorexia nervosa. Often, sufferers have missed out on the normal adolescent stages of social development because of their illness. Start with an event which is relatively non-threatening. Remember you cannot force socialisation and that too much pressure is counterproductive. Stick to gentle encouragement. If it is your partner who has anorexia nervosa, it is important that you do not let your own social life die. As a parent, it may seem inappropriate to still have a hand in arranging your child's social life. However, you may need to break the ice by arranging for old friends to call in and perhaps participate in family outings.

Martina

Martina's parents were aware that she had become isolated from her friends. They made arrangements to leave the house on Saturday evenings and encouraged Martina to invite one or two friends around to watch a video and have a snack.

OBSESSIONS AND COMPULSIONS

It is not uncommon for sufferers with anorexia nervosa to have marked obsessive–compulsive problems. Quite apart from their "obsessive" concern about body weight, size and shape, many have obsessions about such matters as cleanliness, tidiness, contamination, danger and harm. They can also have compulsive rituals such as excessive hand-washing, repeated checking, counting and doing things in a certain way. They may ask repeatedly for reassurance from people who are close to them "Did I do it all right?" "Is it OK if I do not check that again?". It is important that you do not fall into the trap, which is all too easy, of saying "Yes" or "OK". Such responses do not provide reassurance, and perpetuate the cycle. Rather you should say something like: "I will not agree with your obsessional rituals." This will not be easy but remember discomfort now will lead to future improvement.

Mary

Mary, an 18-year-old girl who had anorexia and was treated in hospital did everything in fours. She felt she "had to do this". For example, when she got out of bed in the morning, she would make her bed four times. She would enter any room, including the bathroom, only at the fourth trial, having gone in and come out three times. She was obsessed with the idea that, if she did not do everything in fours, some great harm would come to her family and to herself. She had these problems almost as long as she had the eating difficulties.

Obsessive–compulsive problems usually worsen when the eating problem is severe, and improve with better health. Sometimes, special treatment may be needed. There are things that you can do to help someone with this additional problem. You can encourage the sufferer to try to refrain from the compulsive rituals. Give a clear instruction, then stand firm. For example: "I want you to get dressed now. I will not reassure you when your obsessional side tries to engage me into the obsession/anxiety/reassurance circle." You will feel some discomfort but it will settle. Spending time with her at times when the rituals are most likely, is useful so she can refrain from them with the help of your presence. Remember though, reassurance makes the situation worse. If she repeatedly asks for reassurance, you may say something like: "Didn't we agree not to talk about it?".

Do not be alarmed by the appearance of obsessive–compulsive problems in your daughter or spouse. They do not indicate anything sinister and can be dealt with relatively easily in many cases. Treatments for severe obsessive–compulsive problems are quite effective. For further information about these difficulties read *Obsessive-compulsive disorder* (Padmal de Silva & Stanley Rachman, 1992.)

DEPRESSION

Low mood and depression are consequences of starvation whether they result from famine or are experimentally produced. Several of the men in the Ancel Keys (1950) experiment in Minnesota became very depressed when they lost weight. One or two became so severely depressed that they were taken into hospital.

Many of the depressive symptoms seen in people with anorexia nervosa resemble those in patients with a depressive illness. Thinking and emotions change. Sufferers become sad. They are unable to derive pleasure in the ways they would have previously. Concentration is impaired. They become pessimistic about the future. However, suicidal thoughts are not as common in anorexia nervosa as they are in depression.

It is difficult to distinguish some of the physical features of depression from those of starvation. Poor sleep, fatigue, and physical aches and pains are common to both.

The depression of starvation does not respond easily to antidepressant drugs. These appear to be ineffective at very low weights. Weight gain alone corrects the depression of starvation. In some cases, depression as a form of mental illness and depression as a symptom of starvation coexist. In this case, antidepressants are necessary.

WHAT ABOUT WORK?

Anorexia nervosa has a variety of effects upon work. In severe cases sufferers have to take sick leave because they lack the energy, concentration and stamina necessary for the job. In such cases, it may be necessary to renegotiate a gradual transition back to work.

The sufferer may run into financial difficulties. If you protect your daughter from this you are not helping her to face the reality of her situation.

CONCLUSION

You will have seen from this chapter that there are no hard and fast rules about what you should do as a parent. The best that you can do is to practise the skills of patience and perseverence. Aim to be available as a source of support but also look after yourself as best you can.

On average, anorexia nervosa lasts about 5 years. However, about a quarter of cases have an illness than lasts over 10 years and may remain chronic.

FURTHER READING

de Silva, P., & Rachman, S. (1992). *Obsessive–compulsive disorder: The facts*. Oxford: Oxford University Press.

Keys, A., Brozeck, J., Henschel, A., Michelson, O., & Taylor, A. (1950). *The biology of human starvation*. Minneapolis, MN: University of Minnesota Press.

SECTION THREE
For sufferers

CHAPTER NINE

Preparing yourself to go: Recruiting help

This section is written primarily for the sufferer. This is for people who are beginning to move away from their anorexia nervosa. You may be in the lucky position of being able to work through this section with some professional help. There are obviously some chapters in sections 1 and 2 which will be relevant to you. For example, you may be interested to understand the causes of the illness which you will find in Chapter 2. Also, we recommend you read Chapter 5 which describes the stages you will need to go through when trying to get to grips with your anorexia nervosa. It is probable that because you are reading this you are in the contemplation stage, that is, you think you might have a problem but are undecided. On the other hand, you may even have reached the action stage when you will need as much help as you can get, as you will be fighting on all fronts. There again, you may be in the precontemplation stage if you are reading this because someone asked you to, but you don't think you have a problem.

This section contains the tools you need to get moving. Parents and concerned others may also find this section helpful. The first stage of the work is to ensure that you understand as much as possible of what is going on.

We need to be honest at this point. *Getting over anorexia nervosa often involves getting much worse before you get better.* People may have said to you, if only you would eat this or that, you would be better. In the long term they are right but in the short term this is far from the truth.

Recovery takes a lot of courage and energy. Physically, you may feel awful, your stomach and gut may become bloated and sore, your bones and muscles may ache and psychologically and emotionally you will be on a see-saw. We will go though these difficulties in more detail in Chapter 11.

It is difficult to negotiate this stage alone and we therefore suggest that you find someone to share the task with. It doesn't have to be a family member. But it should be someone who can see you regularly. We have written a checklist of qualities that you should try to look for in your helper.

SUPPORT QUESTIONNAIRE

Could X be your support? Answer the following questions.

1. *How easy is it to talk to X about your problem?*
    Very easy (5 points) quite easy (4 points) not sure (3 points) quite difficult (2 points) very difficult (1 point).
2. *Is X critical or easily upset about your eating? Does X take your eating behaviour personally?*
    Always (1 point) often (2 points) sometimes (3 points) rarely (4 points) never (5 points).
3. *Could you talk to X even if you weren't making progress?*
    Definitely (3 points) not sure (2 points) definitely not (1 point).
4. *Can you trust X to be always there when you need someone—with no strings attached? No moral blackmail?*
    Definitely (5 points) probably (4 points) maybe (3 points) probably not (2 points) definitely not (1 point).
5. *If you overcame your anorexia, what would X's likely response be?*
    (a) X would feel threatened by this. They would have to find a new role and way of living (0 points).
    (b) X would feel lost and slightly jealous that I could become more independent and successful with my life (0 points).
    (c) I haven't a clue (1 point).
    (d) X would be very pleased for me (2 points).
6. *How often are you in contact with X?*
    At least once a week (3 points).
    At least once a fortnight (2 points).
    At least once a month (1 point).
    Less than once a month (0 points).

Total number of points 19–23: You are in the lucky position of having a near perfect supporter nearby. You should definitely ask person X to help you in your efforts to overcome your eating disorder.

Total number of points 12–18: It is uncertain whether X should be your supporter. It is possible that they are too emotionally involved to be of help. It may be too hot an issue.

Total number of points 4–11: Look for someone else or go it alone.

PHASE 1: GETTING GOING

The most difficult step is to let yourself realise that you have a problem. I hope you will have read some of the chapters in Section 1 and in particular the historical one (Chapter 4). If so you will note that not thinking you have a problem is an integral feature of anorexia nervosa. That is, you probably do have anorexia nervosa if you are not worried about yourself when others are! Eventually, most sufferers do come to the stage when they recognise that their life has become strangled by the anorexia minx. At first this idea comes and goes.

It is difficult to do anything about your anorexia until you have fully accepted that your anorexia is a concern for you. This chapter is to help you get to this stage.

One concept that we have found useful is to conceptualise anorexia nervosa as a "minx" that sits on your shoulder and whispers instructions to you about how to behave, etc. Once the idea that an anorexia minx is on your shoulder enters your mind it is important to stay with this thought a little longer. The drawing shows you this image.

Look at it. How does it make you think? How does it make you feel? How does it make you behave? Write down your thoughts. Do you have an image that makes more sense to you? Focus on this for a while. Write about or draw it.

It may help you to get going to see how other people set about this task. This is Julie's example.

Julie

Julie was aged 28. She had developed anorexia nervosa four years earlier. She decided to seek treatment because she and her boyfriend had become more committed to each other. She decided that she ought to seek treatment for her anorexia nervosa before their relationship went further.

After her first session she took the image of the anorexia minx home with her and started to work on it. She structured the way the anorexia minx was affecting her health (physical and psychological) and the way it was affecting her social life (career, family etc.).

How the anorexia minx affects my physical health

1. I'm exhausted all the time and end up falling asleep during the day for a few hours.
2. When I'm working out, my body and muscles are telling me to stop, but I won't. I'm too stubborn.
3. I have headaches all the time. This may be because of dehydration.
4. I feel light-headed all the time. I get faint if I get up too quickly.
5. I don't really sleep very well at nights. I keep waking up every hour.
6. I look pale most of the time.
7. When I've eaten I feel so full that my stomach is distended. I'm afraid to look at it.
8. I do get constipated sometimes.
9. Having a dry mouth all the time makes me feel weak and dirty. I'm always cleaning my teeth.
10. I feel weak and listless all the time and seem to have no energy.
11. Sometimes I feel my arms and legs are just too heavy to lift.
12. I get aches in my joints all the time.

How the anorexia minx is affecting my psychological health

1. I feel I'm too fat even though people tell me the opposite. But I can't see it. I know they are lying and saying it to make me feel better but it doesn't.
2. I have to exercise constantly otherwise I'll have extra blobs where I don't want them. I feel very guilty and annoyed with myself if I don't exercise every day or so.
3. I am very controlled about my diet. I feel very guilty just for eating. I get panicky about it.
4. I feel the need to be very strict with myself.
5. I feel tearful most of the time. I feel I am putting on a front to show people I am fine.
6. I'm very unhappy about myself. I hate myself and I get

depressed about the whole situation.

7. I don't have enough enthusiasm for things anymore. I used to be enthusiastic about everything.
8. I don't have the get up and go I once had. Everything is such an effort now.
9. I have to write everything down or else in 5 minutes or so I forget them.

How the anorexia minx has affected my career
   1. I work part-time at the moment because I'm not fit or strong enough to work full-time. I work in the morning when I'm at my best. In the evenings I'm exhausted.
   2. My career development has been put on hold.

How the anorexia minx has affected relationships
   1. Mother constantly keeps telling me I should eat, but I close my ears to her and do the opposite. I haven't much time for that and try to shut it out.
   2. I have gone off sex with my boyfriend, although I do think about it quite often. I don't want him to see my body and see how big I am. I don't want him put off for life.

How the anorexia minx has affected friendships
   1. I don't really see them that much because I'm too exhausted to go out at night. But sometimes they come round to me.
   2. If I've booked to see them I want to cancel things, thinking I'm not going to enjoy it. Once I'm out I do enjoy myself but it just feels so much of an effort. Yet my friends are very important to me.
   3. I have to psyche myself up to see them. I have to get into the mood/right frame of mind.

Do any of these apply to you? Can you add more to this list?

While you are at this stage another exercise that is useful is to write some letters for yourself. First write a letter to your anorexia nervosa minx as if it were your enemy. Accuse it of causing you problems, be explicit. What troubles has it pulled you into?

Here is an example of a letter written by Jackie

Dear Anorexia (my enemy),
   I have had you dogging my life for over 10 years. You were with me all my student days. Then you made it difficult for me to join in with everyone else. I tended to withdraw to swot. I passed my exams

with distinction but I didn't make any friendships that are still with me. Also I don't seem to be getting on at work now I've qualified. I find it difficult to concentrate and I sometimes miss the point.

All of my peers at college are now marrying and having children. I have never had a relationship. Men just don't seem interested in me. I'm frightened to death of getting too close to them, perhaps they can sense this.

Life is such a struggle. I'm exhausted all the time. It's a nightmare trying to keep warm in the winter. I feel hopeless when I see my life stretching ahead, lonely, irritable and unwell. It's not as if I was expecting too much out of life just a companion and a home and a job that's all.

Yours with regret and anger,
Jackie

How does it make you feel reading Jackie's letter? What do you think she felt when she wrote it? How did it make you feel writing a letter to your anorexia minx enemy? Can you show the letter to someone else and ask for their comments? Would they want to add any more?

Yet another way to focus on this issue is to take yourself to the future, say five years on when you still have anorexia nervosa. Write a letter to a friend describing what your life is like then. How does it make you feel? Show it to a friend. Is this what you really want?

Giving up anorexia will not be easy. Once you have made the decision to struggle with your anorexia minx it will not all be plain sailing. Numerous questions and fears arise. Some of them may get suppressed because they sound silly or unimportant. It is necessary to address even the most trivial of points otherwise they may expand and bowl you over later. You will have very good reasons why recovering from anorexia nervosa is difficult for you, otherwise you would have succeeded before. It is possible that some of the reasons were based on misconceptions. Things might be different now, you may have more resources to think about alternative solutions or know where to get them if you haven't got them yourself. Try to focus on possible obstacles to your recovery. Look at the drawing about the next stage which shows you struggling to pull the anorexia minx off your back.

PHASE 2: STRUGGLING WITH RECOVERY

The following is the work that Annabel undertook when looking at the image of struggling into recovery.

Annabel
Annabel was 17. She had developed anorexia nervosa at the age of 13. She had missed two years' school. Her younger sister was very fed up with the attention and disruption that Annabel's illness had caused the family. Annabel wrote down her thoughts on contemplating the drawing on p. 90.

How shaking off the anorexia minx will affect my psychological health
1. Scared that I'll get so used to eating that I won't be able to stop.
2. I will get out of control.
3. How will I cope with putting on weight and not exercising? Will it go on mainly as fat and not as muscle?
4. I will be frustrated that I am not completely better. I SHOULD be better.
5. I may become more distressed. I sometimes deal with this by increasing my rituals and compulsive actions.

How shaking off the anorexia minx will affect my physical health
1. I might feel very bloated.
2. Worried about the weight not distributing evenly.

How shaking off the anorexia minx will affect my social life
1. Remarks may be made about fattening-up nicely, etc.
2. I may realise I need certain people, or do I?
3. I may get put back in touch with lots of feelings.
4. I may feel embarrassed and not want to see friends when I am in this in-between stage.

How will shaking off the anorexia minx affect my career?
1. Am I clever enough?
2. Am I confident enough?

How will shaking off the anorexia minx affect relationships with my family?

1. A tiny part of me thinks it is giving in to my parents even though I want to put on weight too.
2. They get impatient and think I'm not putting on weight fast enough and it's worse when they don't acknowledge this and go all silent. My mum especially rejects passively.
3. My emotions may well up like a volcano. I may take it out on my family and become very angry.

Do any items on this list ring true for you? What other ones can you add? How does it make you feel, thinking about all the things that will be difficult if you go for recovery?

Another way to concentrate your mind on the issues that you will miss when you have given up anorexia nervosa is to write a letter to the anorexia minx, your friend.

Here is an example of a letter Anne wrote:

Dear Anorexia (my friend),

With you I know where I am. You will never let me down. I know what to think and say. I get a high from remaining in control. It's good to feel special and different and not bothered by things that seem to distract so many others. With you I don't feel lonely, I know how to fill my evenings. You way of life is so familiar to me. How can I ever lose you?

With love,
Anne

How does this letter make you feel? What would you say to Anne to comfort her about the loss of her anorexic friend? How did it feel when you wrote the letter to your anorexic friend? Can you show your letter to your supporter? What do they say about it?

Finally, you need to consider what it will be like when you leave your anorexia behind. Many of you stepped straight from childhood and into anorexia nervosa. You have therefore missed out on a most valuable stage of development, your teenage years. Teenage years are useful as you can try on different attitudes and behaviours before you settle down to your adult self. It can be very frightening to have missed out on this transition stage and to have to pick up an adult persona without preparation. Look at the drawing on page 93 to help you concentrate on what difficulties you anticipate having to contend with when you leave your anorexia nervosa behind.

PHASE 3: WHAT TO EXPECT WITH RECOVERY

What images come to your mind? Write them down and draw them.

Helen
    Helen developed anorexia nervosa at 19 when she left home to train as a radiographer. She was forced to leave her course and returned to live at home. Here are some of the things that Helen was able to think about.

What will happen to my social life when I leave my anorexia minx behind?
    1.   People will no longer worry about me.
    2.   I will be able to be more independent.
    3.   I might feel forgotten about again.

What will happen to my psychological health when I leave the anorexia minx behind?
    1.   I accept that I will not feel good about myself.
    2.   I will get very concerned about my body shape. How will I be able to watch TV without making comparisons?

What will happen to my physical health when I leave my anorexia minx behind?
1.   I won't be cold and tired any more.
2.   I'll get my periods back and feel like a normal woman again.

PREPARING FOR THE REST OF YOUR LIFE

It can be difficult to know what you want to expect from the future when you have had to carry the burden of anorexia for so long. Can you imagine what life would be like without anorexia nervosa? It's difficult to lift your head up and see what will be there. One way to focus your mind is to write a letter to a friend describing the future in five years if all is well and if you have got rid of your anorexia nervosa. If you are having difficulty thinking about five years, shorten the interval, two years, one year, this afternoon!

Here is a letter that Helen wrote:

Dear Susan,

It's difficult to look back and contemplate all the changes that have taken place over the last few years. You will remember how morose and desperate I was when I was in the throes of my anorexia nervosa.

In many ways I learnt a lot from my experience. It gave me a chance to make a fresh start and not do what I thought was expected of me. I had decided on radiography because I thought it would please my mother who had trained as a nurse. However, I had never been very good at science and I found the rote learning of anatomy dreadful.

I realised that I needed to do things to please me rather than try to get other people's approval which never seemed to come my way no matter how hard I tried. I therefore enrolled in a jewellery-making course and then I started to live. I still probably work too hard but its something that I enjoy. I get such a thrill to recycle my profits into new machines which can allow me to try many new techniques.

Another major lesson I learnt from the illness was the need to trust in others and to give them the space and opportunity to show their friendship. I am able to open up a little and share my bad times as well as my good. Its great to realise that people don't think I am selfish or boring if I whine a little. I soon find that my glums vanish after a little sympathy and humour. I ensure that time with friends is given as high a priority as time in my workshop.

I guess many people will think that my eating habits are a little on the weird side but I am able to ensure that my size 12 clothes never get too loose on me. I've abandoned scales, diets and cults of thinness. My relationship with my parents has improved. I know that they don't approve totally of my lifestyle but we have tacitly agreed to disagree. I don't feel I have to rub their noses in my rebellious acts neither do I have to do everything they ask.

Let yourself daydream. Imagine you are given three wishes. What would you like to see happen if you didn't have anorexia nervosa? Once you can imagine your life without anorexia nervosa, practise getting into this fantasy each day. At first, just practise doing it while you are lying in bed. Go back to the same scene each night and add some more on to the image. How does the image make you feel? If you feel slightly frightened or distressed bring a friend into your image who will be able to make you feel at ease. Gradually practise this technique. Imagine yourself successfully making a start on loosening the stranglehold of anorexia nervosa next month, next week, tomorrow.

Once you have finished this chapter you should be better informed about yourself and your anorexia. What can you conclude? Are you at the stage when you know it is a problem and want to do something about it? If so, can you say it out loud so that you can hear yourself say it? What about sharing it with someone else?

If you feel that you can't do anything about it yet can you ensure that you are treading water and not getting sucked further in? Can you write this down or share it with someone else?

If you feel totally engulfed can you talk to someone else about it so that you can get extra help? Can you let your family help more? Can you go to a day centre? What about admission to hospital? Can you arrange some respite care? Some forms of anorexia nervosa are so severe that repeated admission to hospital is necessary. Do not see this as failure. Sometimes it is necessary to go around the wheel of change many times.

CHAPTER TEN

Understanding
yourself

Anorexia nervosa often gets established as a way of coping with a difficult situation. Your mind becomes filled with anorexia nervosa and food, and so the problem is successfully blocked out. This may give you an initial sense of relief as unpleasant things can be shut out. However, just because you are no longer aware of the problem, doesn't mean that it is not still there. It may be hidden deeply. Sometimes, the original problem has gone but you may unconsciously act as if it is still there. If you find there is a problem that you may have been trying to avoid, try to use the steps detailed in Chapter 6 to tackle it.

1.   Clearly define the problem.
2.   Brainstorm—think of solutions.
3.   Weigh up position.
4.   Choose an option.
5.   Review.

Here are some examples of problems that others have been able to define.

Alison
Alison's parents both had careers in show business in their youth. They had long since retired but had fond memories of that time. As a child, Alison showed talent as a dancer. She succeeded in

getting into stage school. Once she had qualified she found that jobs were difficult to secure. She went to audition after audition. The stories she heard from colleagues were very depressing. Those who had got jobs in the West End frequently found that their job ended without notice. She met the same people going round and round. Nevertheless, her parents encouraged her to persist, telling her what a good life it was. In counselling, Alison was able to think about herself and her situation. She was freed from the automatic assumptions and expectations of her family. When she wrote her letter to the future, dancing was notable by its absence. Instead, she talked about having a husband and home. It was as if at the back of her mind she knew that a career in dancing was not what she wanted. On the other, she wanted to please her parents who had done so much for her. Her anorexia nervosa seemed to release her from this dilemma because it was apparent to everyone that she was too ill to go to auditions. Her skeletal frame put everybody off. She therefore didn't have to confront her parents with her doubts about her proposed career. Alison was able to identify her problem: "I do not want a career in dancing, only my parents want it." She thought of options: (1) to go on auditioning for dancing, (2) to think of other careers, (3) to try to talk her parents round.

Alison was able to express her concerns about dancing and have them listened to in counselling. She was gradually able to have the space to think about a career that did not include dancing. Gradually she was able to express these doubts to her parents. At first they resisted the idea and argued against any change in plan. However, Alison was able to propose that she try an alternative career for an experimental phase and gradually they came round to this idea. Alison quickly succeeded in getting a job in insurance and was quickly promoted. Slowly she was able to fight off her anorexia. Her parents accepted her decision and were delighted when she was able to make good progress in her new career

Ruth

Ruth's parents had regularly argued during her childhood. Her dad tended to spend most of his time at the golf club or at work. Her mother walked out taking the children with her and returned to her parents' home at one stage.

When Ruth developed anorexia nervosa she found that her parents became close. The arguments stopped and her father cut down his visits to the golf course and came home to be with Ruth. It was as if Ruth was frightened of getting better because she feared her parents would revert to their previous patterns. Ruth needed a period of inpatient treatment. It required a lot of time before she was able to discuss how her illness seemed to bring about a welcome change in the family. It was difficult for her to acknowledge that there were family problems. She was reluctant to talk, as it seemed disloyal. However, she was able to identify the problem: "My parents do not get on well. They may separate." Her options were: (1) continue to try to keep her parents together by her behaviour, (2) realise that she could not be responsible for her parents, and accept that she would have to get on with her own life, (3) tell them to separate. She chose option 2. Once Ruth saw this pattern she began to contemplate moving out of her home. She avoided getting drawn in to discussions about the other parent. She would interrupt any conversation that started this way by saying: "I do not want to be involved in discussions about Dad/Mum when he/she is not present. If you want to talk to me about it I suggest that we all meet together but I would prefer not to be involved unless necessary."

Sally

Sally's parents were both busy professionals. Her older brother, Mark, was the golden boy. He had represented his county for cricket. He had academic success and had gone on to Oxford. Sally always felt overshadowed by him. Her parents had seemed to spend all their spare time watching him play cricket or collect prizes. Once Sally developed anorexia nervosa she was aware that, for once in her life, she held her parents' attention. They visited her in hospital, her mother reduced her hours at work to spend more time with her. One of Sally's fears was that if she got better then she would be forgotten again. Sally found it very difficult to admit this feeling directly. She merely hinted at it. Eventually she was able to accept her problem: "I will get ignored unless I am ill." She thought about her options: (1) to remain the same, (2) to develop a circle of friends who shared a common enjoyment in life, (3) to go to navigation classes so that she could crew boats with her father. She decided to try for options 2 and 3. Gradually, she developed a network of friends through her own efforts and through friends of her father.

Many people seem to slip into anorexia nervosa when they are confronting distressing emotions. At first this is very rewarding as the distress appears to go immediately. Unfortunately, the distress can be retriggered very easily and gets more intense each time it surfaces. This leads to more frantic attempts to regain control which leads to more anorexia nervosa and a vicious circle begins. When faced with strong emotions,we do know that it is important to let them run their course. They will gradually decrease and more positive emotions will return. If you attempt to disrupt this process by blocking, controlling or generally trying to get rid of unpleasantness it will only serve to kindle severe protracted distress. This of course is recognised in common lore. The function of the wake at a funeral was to express feelings of loss and abandonment there and then. In our culture we value a stiff upper lip and are puzzled by cultures that weep and wail, and yet we are exposed to more events that make us sad such as the breakdown of families. Because we are seduced into feeling that we have tamed nature we feel failures if things go wrong.

Can you identify any difficulties that you will need to face if you try to leave your anorexia minx behind? Were there any problems that just seemed to disappear when your anorexia developed? Try to pare your problem down to the bone. What exactly is the difficulty? Perhaps there is more than one? Separate them out into their simplest forms. Why don't you try to brainstorm some alternatives? If you have some perfectionistic traits you will not find this easy. Perhaps you could ask a friend to help you. Take it in turns to add in another option. Make it playful by adding wacky creations.

Perhaps you don't have any idea if there are problems you are avoiding by your anorexia nervosa, as it may have been such a good smoke-screen. Perhaps you could ask a friend if she had any ideas. Maybe you will never know. Maybe there never was a problem.

WHAT IS ME? WHAT IS STARVATION?

One of the most difficult things about anorexia nervosa is that it invades every part of you: your thinking, your feelings, and your body. It can strangle the real you like convolvulus. One of the first tasks is for you to decide what is you and what is the anorexia nervosa.

The physical effects of starvation lock you into vicious circles. Problems and vulnerabilities produce anorexia. Lack of food leads to starvation. Starvation weakens the body and spirit so that it is impossible to fight the problems. This circularity between weight loss as a cause of problems, as well as a consequence of the illness is something that may be difficult to break.

It is difficult to know where the anorexia ends and starvation begins. The Minnesota study led by Ancel Keys (1950) which was referred to earlier, can help distinguish the two different aspects. The men who underwent a period of experimental weight loss described their experiences. They did not have anorexia nervosa, therefore their experiences were due to starvation alone. Do any of these resonate with you?

For a few weeks the new life was fun. I was losing weight of course, but I still had a lot of energy. Then came the day when I lost my 'will to activity'. I no longer cared to do anything that required energy and days began to drag—each day getting longer and longer and there seemed no end of starvation in sight. Six months were an eternity. But they went by; slowly, slowly. I would compare my reflection in the mirror with that of my picture in pre-starvation days. My hair was thinner, eyes looked hollow, cheeks were only thin coverings for the bones of my face. When I tried to smile it was a grimace and I didn't feel like smiling and never laughed. My muscles were almost gone, my bones protruded (even a few seconds of sitting on a hard chair were uncomfortable) and my skin was grey and lustreless. A quarter of my original body weight had been consumed for energy during this period of deficiency. I felt as old as the aged men on my hospital ward.

How does it feel to starve? It is something like this:

I'm hungry. I'm always hungry—not like the hunger that comes when you miss lunch, but a continual cry from the body for food. At times I can almost forget about it but there is nothing that can hold my interest for long. I wait for mealtimes. When it comes I eat slowly and make the food last as long as possible. The menu never gets monotonous even if it is the same each day or is of poor quality. It is food and all food tastes good. Even dirty crusts of bread in the street looks appetizing and I envy the fat pigeons picking at them and the sight of people wasting it in restaurants is intolerable.

I'm cold. In July I walk downtown on a sunny day with a shirt and sweater on to keep me warm. At night my well-fed room mate, who isn't in the experiment sleeps on top of his sheets but I crawl under two blankets wondering why Don isn't freezing to death. My body flame is burning as low as possible to conserve precious fuel and still maintaining life processes.

I'm weak. I can walk miles at my own pace to satisfy laboratory requirements, but often I trip on cracks in the side walks. To open a heavy door it is necessary to brace myself and push or pull with all my might. I wouldn't think of trying to throw a baseball and I couldn't jump over a twelve-inch railing if I tried. The lack of strength is a great frustration. In fact it is often a greater frustration than the hunger. I eagerly look forward to the day when I can go upstairs two at a time or maybe run to catch a street car.

And now I have oedema. When I wake up in the morning my face is puffy on the side I was lying on. Sometimes my ankles swell and my knees are puffy, but my oedema isn't as bad as that of several others whose flesh bulges out over their shoes in the evening. Social graces, interests, spontaneous activity and responsibility take second place to concerns of food. I lick my plate unashamedly at each meal even when guests are present. I don't like to sit near guests, for then it is necessary to entertain and talk with them. That takes too much energy and destroys some of the enjoyment that comes from my food. I no longer have the desire to help millions of starving people; rather I feel akin to them and hope that I, as well as they, will benefit from scientific refeeding.

I am one of about three or four who still go out with girls. I fell in love with a girl during the control period but I only see her occasionally now. It's almost too much trouble to see her even if she visits me in the Lab. It requires great effort to hold her hand. Entertainment must be tame. If we see a show, the most interesting part is contained in scenes where people are eating. I couldn't laugh at the funniest picture in the world, and love scenes are completely dull.

I can talk intellectually, my mental ability has not decreased, but my will to use my ability has. So my talk is of food and past memories, or future ambitions mostly in the cooking or eating line.

He then goes on to describe what happened when the experiment ended and they were allowed to gain weight.

That was starvation! Rehabilitation was carried on with the same food only more of it, but life came back slowly. The men were divided into four groups. I was in the lowest group and after 6 weeks of refeeding had gained one quarter of a pound! I felt better, however, as many pounds of oedema had been replaced by healthy tissues. At the end of 6 weeks everyone was given an additional 800 calories daily. Now men in the lowest group were getting 3000 calories (about the average daily amount of the American diet) but even on this diet the average weight gain in their group twelve weeks after the end of starvation was only 7½ pounds compared with nearly a 40pound average loss. Now eight months after the end of starvation, I am fat and healthy although my muscles have not yet returned to their former tone. I look back to those days in July and recall my feeling of apathy.

Does any of this description ring true for you? This essay is very useful as it clearly defines the effects of lack of food alone. So often in other situations of starvation, such as famines or prisoner of war camps, the effects are compounded by disease. In the next section we consider how you may be trapped by spirals of starvation.

1. Physical disability.   The physical complications of anorexia nervosa include weakness associated with starvation or salt or hormonal imbalance (described vividly in the earlier passage). These may heighten your sense of vulnerability or personal inadequacy, especially when you do not accept you are ill. You may view these impairments as further evidence of "personal weakness" and intensify your efforts at achieving self-control by dieting more rigorously. A self-defeating vicious cycle is started.

2. Emotional disturbances.   Physical processes in your brain and hormones associated with weight loss can lead to emotional disturbances such as depression and irritability. You may attempt to deal with these "unacceptable" aspects of yourself by escalating your "anorexic" behaviours.

Compulsive behaviours and thoughts are a feature of starvation. In conditions of famine this has some survival advantages. Unfortunately, in anorexia nervosa this compulsive drive is often focused on anorexic behaviours. You may feel compelled to exercise more and more, or to chop your food into smaller and smaller pieces.

3. Effects on the brain.   Mental function is affected by weight loss, as was discussed by the Minnesota volunteer. Concentration, attention, memory, learning and problem-solving are impaired. These effects may cloud your judgement. It is difficult to have rational thoughts about the illness and about problems in general. Your problem-solving capabilities will be impaired. You will not be able to generate as many solutions when you "brainstorm". You may not be able to take the steps required to implement any solution. Your thinking will become even more black and white. Your ability to use and benefit from psychological treatments requiring, as they do, new learning and flexibility in thinking, may be curtailed, reducing further the changes of recovery. Insight into the effects of the illness and the need for treatment may be lost. Recovery of brain function and agility is slow. Do not despair, it can return.

4. Effects on your social life.   Your preoccupation with food (a starvation effect) limits your ability to take part in social events. This was clearly illustrated in the essay earlier. You lose your interest in friendships and general topics. You lose your sense of humour. Friends become bored and drift away. Loss of your social network will heighten your feelings of alienation and distress. Unfortunately, you will be tempted to deal with this with more anorexic behaviour.

5. Effect on your digestive system.   You will find that meals are highly distressing with mixed emotions of panic, guilt and uncomfortable physical sensations. You may have developed a conditioned aversion to some foodstuffs. Conditioning occurs when the mind learns to link an event (e.g. eating a bar of chocolate) with distressing consequences such as the image of swelling up to elephantine proportions. Even the sight of a chocolate bar can then lead to panic. The longer and more completely are chocolate bars eschewed, the more firmly is this new learning set down. Your mind is not given the opportunity to learn that "death by chocolate" does not really occur. Fats are the foodstuffs now commonly linked to calamitous consequences.

You will also develop physical distress in your gut. "Bloating" or rapid fullness is due in part to a delay in emptying of your stomach. You may become preoccupied with the thought that your stomach is swelling up like a balloon after a meal. This is because the muscles from the abdominal wall have been eaten away during the starvation and your abdominal wall therefore sags. Also, muscle from the gut wall itself is lost. This means the gut swells up with wind and fluid more than usual.

6. Hormones.   Loss of your sex hormones from starvation can be a mixed blessing. Your sexual fantasising may stop. Your yearnings for a physical relationship vanish. This can make life very simple. You are not driven by your hormones into relationships. However, this can lead to you feeling different to everyone else, left as a bit of a gooseberry. It may add to feelings of being defective in some way.

7. Changes in body composition.   You will have lost bone, brain and muscle tissue. These losses are invisible to the naked eye but can be seen by special X-rays. It may be difficult to accept that you need to gain weight as your body is still functioning.

FURTHER READING

Keys, A., Brozeck, J., Henschel, A., Michelson, O., & Taylor, H. (1950). *The biology of human starvation*. Minneapolis, MN: University of Minnesota Press.

CHAPTER ELEVEN

What are the dangers of anorexia nervosa?

It was difficult to know where to place this chapter. Using earlier drafts of this book I have asked various sufferers, carers, and professionals who work in the field for their advice and comments. The response was mixed. Some people felt that it was too medical and should be in the therapist section, while others felt that sufferers needed to be kept informed. I finally decided to keep it here as I prefer an open collaborative relationship, but be warned, this chapter may be too distressing or technical for you. Feel free to skip it!

In order to get better you need to gain weight as your body is experiencing the effects of starvation. To appreciate the seriousness of the illness, it is important to understand the effect starvation has on your body and the dangers involved.

THE RISK OF DEATH

Anorexia nervosa is a serious illness. Although it may be distasteful, it is important to consider the risks of death. It is a tragedy when a young life is lost through anorexia nervosa. You may have no warning. Young women with anorexia nervosa have even died in hospital.

Susan

Susan had had anorexia for two years. She had been referred for treatment to a specialised unit but they had no beds. She was admitted to a medical ward, but she was easily able to outsmart the busy nurses and not eat. Her weight fell and she was found dead in her bed one evening and could not be resuscitated.

Martine

Martine was a 29-year-old solicitor who had struggled with her eating disorder for over 10 years. Her vomiting had become more severe under the strain of a new job. She decided to make an appointment to see a specialist. The week before she went to clinic she suddenly collapsed. She was dead on arrival in casualty; her potassium level was very low.

The tragedy of deaths that occur in anorexia nervosa is that the sufferer may be unable to understand that she is putting her life at such risk. She truly believes that she can live on nothing.

Alternatively, thinking may be distorted by other mistaken beliefs. For example, someone who has been distressed with anorexia nervosa for a long time may believe that both she and her family would be better off if she were dead. Neither of these is, of course, true. We know that parents who lose a child never get over the death, it always remains as a wound to them. Also, although we do not know for certain that death does not lead to absence of pain and distress, many wise people who have thought about these matters suggest that this mode of death may lead to a condition of continuing pain. Records of near-death experiences in this situation appear to confirm this. However, the risk of death with anorexia nervosa is real, and is sixteen times that of the normal population rate. The general health hazards are even more common.

HEALTH HAZARDS OF STARVATION

A. The effects of starvation on the body

1. Sensitivity to cold: poor circulation results in hands and feet becoming blue, mottled, swollen and subject to chilblains. Some women with anorexia nervosa have died of hypothermia.
2. Sleep disturbances: waking up early or several times in the night.
3. Weak bladder: passing water frequently throughout the day or night.
4. Excess hair growth on the body, particularly on the back, and the sides of the face.

5. Poor circulation, slow pulse, low blood pressure and fainting spells.
6. Thin bones (osteoporosis): with time, this may result in fracture leading to deformity and pain.
7. Periods stop or become very irregular. It is usually only possible for a woman to have periods when 15% of her body is composed of fat.
8. The stomach shrinks and feels uncomfortably distended after eating even a small amount of food, stomach ulcers may be a problem which persists after recovery.
9. Gut function is slowed and constipation results.
10. The bone marrow fails. Red and white blood cells are not formed quickly enough which results in anaemia and susceptibility to certain infections.
11. The lack of nutrition affects the liver so that it is unable to manufacture body proteins. This may result in swelling of the ankles and legs.
12. Blood cholesterol level is *increased*. This results from the lack of oestrogen (women before their menopause are protected from heart attacks by oestrogen) from abnormal liver function.
13. Nerves and muscles become damaged. This may make it difficult to climb stairs, the feet may drag, and extreme fatigue and tiredness supervenes.
14. In young children, growth may be stunted and puberty delayed (see pp. 112–113).
15. Low glucose: this produces sensations of panic or light-headedness. If ignored, this can lead to coma and death.
16. The kidney is prone to infection and stone formation and may eventually fail.

How many of these symptoms have you experienced? Not only does your body have to cope with starvation it also has to cope with various weight control methods.

Exercise
This is the commonest form of weight control in patients with anorexia nervosa. This may be obvious, such as walking and jogging throughout the day, or may be done more secretively. When weight loss is severe and energy reserves depleted, overexercise can lead to dangerously low sugar levels. This can lead to coma and death. The wear and tear on the body can cause problems. As the bones are thin, stress fractures emerge. Muscles and joints can be damaged from increased strain. Sometimes, the drive to exercise is motivated by the need to keep in shape.

Overexercise, in the context of starvation, destroys muscle and hence shape, as your body eats up your own flesh. You cannot expect to tone up if you do not have muscle fibres present.

Think of Black Beauty. If you remember, at one stage in his life he was underfed and forced to pull a coal waggon. He collapsed and nearly died. It doesn't just happen to animals. The mortality among the Japanese prisoner of war victims was increased because they were forced to work on the railways as well as being starved.

Vomiting and laxatives

Self-induced vomiting, laxative abuse or other extreme methods of weight control increase the health risks. In particular, there is damage to the teeth, kidney and gut. These other methods of weight control are particularly damaging and difficult to shake off because they set up vicious circles.

Vomiting can erode the enamel on the teeth, leading to dental decay and increased sensitivity. It can lead to water and salt imbalance which may disturb the function of the heart, brain and kidney. You may interpret feelings of weakness as due to your own lack of control, leading to further attempts to gain control, a vicious circle. Potassium levels can become very low and disturb the electrical activity of the heart and brain leading to heart attacks and fits. The glands in the face can swell up; this can be painful. Also, this rounding of the face will make you believe that you have become fatter which will only make you try to control your weight more, another vicious circle. In some people vomiting can cause tears in the stomach which lead to life-threatening bleeding. The body is not fooled by vomiting, it registers that it has no food available for metabolism and so the hunger drives are stepped up, yet another vicious circle.

Like vomiting, the use of laxatives can lead to serious water and salt imbalance. This also leads to large weight fluctuations. Severe dehydration can lead to kidney failure or kidney stones. Laxatives also damage the bowel, preventing it from working normally, resulting in severe constipation and gassy distension. Straining due to use of laxatives results in piles and prolapse.

Abuse of other medications

You may have been tempted to abuse diet pills and diuretics (elimination of water tablets), either obtained from slimming clinics or health food shops. Diuretics cause dehydration and salt imbalance and hence damage the circulation and kidneys in a similar way to laxatives and vomiting. Diet pills taken to excess cause the body to become overactive and excitable. It can be difficult to sleep. You become on edge and jumpy.

The mind becomes overactive and you become suspicious and agitated. Eventually, epileptic fits develop.

Medical investigations

The doctors helping you get over your anorexia nervosa will do a variety of medical tests and investigations to check your health.

1. *Blood cell count.* A common investigation looks at cells in the blood, red cells, white cells and platelets. If these are abnormal, it may indicate that the bone marrow is failing. This failure is due to inadequate nutrition, and reverses given an adequate food intake. The first cells to be affected are white cells. These are the cells that fight infection, either by killing or disabling germs. The normal white cell count is $4-11 \times 1000$ per millilitre. In anorexia nervosa the level fall may be as low as 1000 per millilitre. Obviously this has implications for the body's resistance to disease. Paradoxically, the common cold occurs less often in very underweight individuals but this is more than balanced by an increase in severe life-threatening illnesses.

The next cell to become involved is the red cell. This is the cell that carries oxygen around the body and attached to the haemoglobin molecule. A reduced haemoglobin level is known as anaemia which leads to tiredness, breathlessness and exhaustion. In severe anorexia nervosa the level of haemoglobin can fall from the normal range of 13–15g/l, to 6g/l. The platelet level decreases in severe states of starvation. Platelets are important in repairing damage to small blood vessels, and take part in the clotting process. If platelet levels are decreased the small blood vessels become leaky and tiny bruises form under the skin. This leads to a rash like measles. All of these changes in the bone marrow and the blood cells reverse once nutrition is adequate. Calories alone are necessary in most cases. Sometimes, iron and vitamins are also needed.

2. *Blood salts.* The commonest and most important abnormality in blood chemistry is a low level of potassium. The normal range is 3.5–5.5mmol/l. Potassium chloride is an important salt in the body cells. The level falls if there is vomiting, diarrhoea (a result of laxatives) or use of diuretics (water tablets). In some cases the level falls to as low as 2mmol/l. Potassium in the blood effects the electrical activity in cell membranes. All cells become weaker because of this. Muscles do not work well and become weak. One of the most important affected organs is the heart, as the electrical activity of the heart is responsible for making the heart beat. If the electrical activity become disrupted the rhythm of the heart changes leading to palpitations or heart attacks. The kidney also suffers, and mental confusion is a common feature.

Loss of potassium is associated with an increased bicarbonate level in the blood. The normal level of bicarbonate is between 20–28mmol/l. Some patients with anorexia nervosa, complicated by vomiting or use of laxatives, have levels of bicarbonate as high as 40mmol/l. High bicarbonate level makes the blood very alkaline and this can effect the distribution of salts. One effect of this is spasm of the hands. In severe cases, epileptic fits can develop.

Laxative abuse can also lead to low levels of plasma sodium, less than 130mmol/l (the normal range is 135–145mmol/l). The cause of the low sodium is often dehydration. In some cases thirst can be absent although the mouth is dry. Low sodium can lead to weakness and faints. Muscle cramps are common. Mental apathy also occurs. Muscle twitching, convulsions and coma may arise.

Other minerals in the body, such as calcium, magnesium and phosphates can also be abnormal.

What can be done? The most obvious answer is to stop doing whatever it is that is causing the abnormality in the first place. Plan to reduce the amount of vomiting perhaps by instituting careful self-supervision. Stop taking laxatives and diuretics. Rapid medical replacement of the deficiencies is usually not the answer. These losses have developed slowly and the body has adapted; if rapid correction with drips of salts into the blood system occurs it may dangerously tip the precarious balance. Similarly, it is best to replace the salts within natural foods rather than in tablet form. Foods rich in potassium include oranges, bananas and other fruits, nuts, Bovril, Marmite, chocolate and coffee.

3. *Blood Chemistry.* Blood tests can also provide information about other systems of the body. Much of the food we eat is processed in the liver, and it is useful to look at its activity in anorexia nervosa. The liver becomes damaged with severe undernutrition and its cells break down, releasing enzymes into the blood. Liver enzymes such as alkaline phosphatase, gamma-glutamyl transaminase may all be increased. Alkaline phosphatase may be increased in younger patients during weight gain when bone turnover is increased.

Cholesterol levels are often raised above 7mmol/l, this is somewhat paradoxical given the low fat diet that you may be on. The exact explanation for this is unknown although it probably relates to abnormal metabolism. If you gain weight by introducing more fats into your diet your cholesterol level will fall.

Blood glucose levels can fall in severe anorexia nervosa and this can lead to death. There have been reports of this occurring without warning, particularly in the context of excessive exercise.

4. *Bone Density*. Patients with bulimia nervosa and anorexia nervosa have been found to have reduced bone density. This is of relevance as it can increase the risk of fracture. Some fractures, such as those of the vertebral column, cannot heal without deformity and so the effects are permanent. The degree of bone loss relates to the degree of weight loss and duration of illness. It is uncertain if full recovery of the bones is possible, particularly if the illness began before puberty. One of the major factors that influence bone density is nutrition, that is, the number of calories and how much calcium and vitamin D is available.

Bone density can be measured with special machines. Not every hospital has them and the test is very expensive. At the moment it is uncertain how much more information such a scan can give.

Once again, the best treatment is probably weight gain. It also makes sense to eat foods that contain calcium. These include milk, cheese, nuts and pulses.

5. *Sex and reproduction*. One of the major markers of an eating disorder in women is the loss of periods. This is just the tip of the iceberg as all aspects of sexual function are affected. The reproductive organs in your body will shrink in size and structure to those of a child before puberty. Without the hormonal environment associated with maturity your sexual drive will also go. You may remember that, when you first heard about sex as a child, it seemed rather dirty and disgusting—"How can my parents do that?". Your sexual drive will diminish and sex may seem rather boring, intrusive and unpleasant. You will no longer have sexual fantasies. You will have no urge to masturbate or have sex. If you are in a relationship this can cause problems. You may feel obliged to please your partner and have sex. Because you have reduced levels of sexual hormones your vagina will be dry and sex may be painful.

What about men? What happens to your sexual function if you are a man with anorexia nervosa? As in women, your sexuality will regress both psychologically and physically. An obvious manifestation of the physical effects is that you will no longer wake up with an erection in the morning. You will fail to get aroused by sexual stimuli which may have excited you in the past.

Tony

Tony developed anorexia nervosa when he was 22. He had had two relationships with girls but had felt very lacking in confidence and they had never developed into a sexual relationship. He developed anorexia nervosa after some stress at work. He noted that he no longer had erections. He interpreted this as failure of his masculinity. He thought that he had become impotent and that his sexual life was over. He was surprised and reassured when his therapist told him that this was a side effect of starvation and that his potency would return with weight gain.

One of the men in the Ancel Keys study of starvation (see Chapter 10), described this loss of sexual appetite with starvation "I feel no more like sex than would a sick oyster".

As referred to in the previous chapter, starvation also has effects on the brain and on behaviour and some of these are detailed below.

B.   The effects of starvation on the mind

1.   Mood is lowered and depression results in pessimism, hopelessness and inability to take pleasure out of life.
2.   The mind becomes preoccupied with food and there is often a strong urge to overeat.
3.   The ability and interest in forming relationships is diminished. Friendships are lost. There is a feeling of being cut-off or isolated from others.
4.   Concentration is poor. It is difficult to work to full capacity.
5.   Minor problems appear insurmountable.
6.   Complex thought is impaired. It is difficult to hold several threads of thought in place at once.

These lists are dry and dull but many authors have written about the effects of starvation, albeit usually not self-imposed. We suggest you read: *One day in the life of Ivan Denisovich* by Alexander Solzhenitsyn, *Slaughterhouse five* by Kurt Vonnegut, and *Castaway* by L. Irvin, to see how starvation affects human thinking and behaviour.

WILL THERE BE PERMANENT DAMAGE?

A question that arises whenever the physical complications are discussed is: "What will be the long-term problems?". It is difficult to answer this with confidence, as there have been relatively few studies which have followed the health of sufferers over time. Most of the physical problems do reverse with weight gain, or if the weight control practices stop. It may depend upon factors such as the duration of illness and the stage of life at which the illness arose. For example, there may be a critical time during which puberty can take place. If the illness strikes before all the stages of puberty have been attained and recovery is delayed, there may be irreversible failure to achieve growth in stature, peak bone density, and secondary sexual development.

The reproductive system is so obviously affected that many people are concerned about the long-term effects. It is probable that, if there is full recovery, then all will return to normal although it may take longer than normal to conceive. In some cases, it may be necessary to have hormonal treatment. The difficulty is that between one-third and one-half of all sufferers may have residual problems and are still under their optimal weight. It is in this group that there may be difficulties with poor fertility or an increase in the rate of miscarriages and problems during pregnancy.

We do not know by how much bone density recovers. There is some evidence that with a short illness the bones can regain their strength and thickness. It may take a long time for the repairs to be completed and some sites are repaired before others. Recovery may be incomplete. If bones remain thin, the risk of fracture is increased. Bones in the spinal column may be crushed because they are thin and fragile and the subsequent loss of height and spinal curvature are irrecoverable. This may lead to chronic pain.

The long-term effects on the heart and circulation are also unknown. In the general population "yo-yo" dieting is associated with an increased risk of cardiovascular disease and death. Patients on very low fat diets often have raised levels of cholesterol, we do not know if this is a risk factor.

After recovery, gut problems can remain. Heartburn and stomach ulcers are more common. The bowel can become "irritable" with frequent diarrhoea or severe constipation.

Weight control measures that alter salt and water balance can lead to permanent kidney damage. As the kidneys have a lot of reserve function this may not become apparent unless they are put under further stress.

OVERVIEW

Anorexia nervosa is a potentially life-threatening condition. The long list of complications may have made you feel very worried and frightened, or even angry and guilty that you are at such a risk. However, information about these serious and severe physical complications may help improve your motivation in the struggle for recovery. Beware of falling into despair and thinking that it only makes the future seem even more hopeless. The aim of this book is not to depress you but to provide you with the facts you need. Other symptoms, particularly psychological ones, usually improve strikingly with refeeding. Treatment, in the absence of weight gain, has little impact on the disorder. No matter how uncomfortable and difficult, it is important to be aware that one of the primary goals is to gain weight.

FURTHER READING

Irvin, L. (1984). *Castaway.* Harmondsworth, UK: Penguin.

Solzhenitsyn, A. (1974). *One day in the life of Ivan Denisovich.* Harmondsworth, UK: Penguin.

Vonnegut, K. (1991). *Slaughterhouse five.* London: Vintage.

CHAPTER TWELVE

What you should know about nutrition and body composition

WHAT YOU SHOULD KNOW ABOUT WEIGHT CONTROL

What is a reasonable weight?

In assessing what is a healthy weight it is important to account for height. Medically, one of the best and simplest methods of doing this is to calculate the body mass index (BMI). The BMI is weight in kilograms divided by the height in metres squared. The healthy BMI range is 20–25. If we define health as lowest mortality then we find that the healthy range increases with age. The lowest mortality is at BMI 19.5kg/m^2 for women at age 20 and 27.3kg/m^2 at age 60.

In Table 12.1, we have given the normal range of BMI which is between $20\text{–}25\text{kg/m}^2$. The World Health Organisation (1990) sets a BMI of 17.5kg/m^2 as the threshold for anorexia nervosa. A BMI of 13.5kg/m^2 is a critical level of weight loss at which admission to hospital should be considered.

You can see from the table that a wide range of weights is normal. At least half of the population are, by definition, in the top half of the range. Interestingly, the fittest people are often in the top half of the range because muscle tissue is quite dense, much denser and heavier than fat, for example. One of the major variables affecting body weight and composition is genetic make-up. Some people are born with a bigger and stronger skeletal frame and the muscles to go with it.

TABLE 12.1
Normal, anorexic and dangerous weights

Height m (ft)	1.52m (5'0")	1.57m (5'2")	1.63m (5'4")	1.68m (5'6")	1.73m (5'8")
Normal range BMI 20–25	45–56kg 46–58kg	48–60kg 49–62kg	51–64kg 53–66kg	54–68kg 56–71kg	58–72kg 60–75kg
Anorexia Nervosa BMI < 17.5	40kg	43kg	47kg	49kg	52kg
Medical danger BMI < 13.5	31kg	33kg	36kg	38kg	40kg

Weight control

Bodily systems are designed to maintain a steady internal state. These rules apply to body composition and weight. Weight loss leads to powerful counterbalancing forces to restore body mass. However, the control of body weight is more complex than, say, the control of blood oxygen level, in that it involves a motivational state, appetite, and food-seeking behaviour. Also the system is not symmetrical. The mechanisms to prevent weight loss are more powerful than those which prevent weight gain. This can be understood in terms of the threats to human life in the past when starvation was more common.

Sanders and Bazalgette, in their book *You don't have to diet*, draw an analogy between the attempts of dieters to control their appetite with a scenario in which it is fashionable to control breathing:

> Imagine for a moment that some scientist claimed that we breathe too much and that we should all hold our breath to lower our blood pressure. Imagine that this point of view was taken up enthusiastically by the newspapers, who encouraged us to breathe less and develop blue complexions. Suppose that blue complexions then became fashionable—fashion models almost stopped breathing altogether and the rest of us, women in particular, tried to do the same.
>
> The trend would spread rapidly. Soon women would be attending 'Breathwatchers' and teenagers would be trying to suffocate themselves in their bedrooms. Other guilty people, despite their desperate desire to be blue, would indulge in breathing 'binges' and lose all grip of their self-control. Inevitably, racketeers would move in with magical pills that would reduce our appetite for air, cans of 'lite' air for 'that blue look', exercises to take

away our craving for oxygen and tight bands to wear round the chest to restrict the size of our inhalations.

'Breath Control' would soon grow into a billion-dollar industry. Women who had achieved really blue complexions would boast, 'I feel like a new person', and gain in self-confidence as they were showered with compliments. No longer would they be ashamed of an ugly pink complexion. Men would find them attractive because they would resemble the sensuous blue skinned models appearing in girlie and fashion magazines.

Everyone has some conscious control over their breathing and can stop it for a while, but eventually the body simply takes over, and breathing begins again; not normal, measured breathing, but gasping for great gulps of air, in a way that is quite out of voluntary control. This provides a clear picture of what Ancel Keys found in his study of starvation in normal men (see Chapter 10). Many men were unable to co-operate with this study and cheated by obtaining food from elsewhere. Those who stuck to the rules binged when they were allowed food. One or two ate so much they had to go into hospital to have their stomachs decompressed. Dietary restriction leads to loss of control, overeating, as a normal, healthy, biological survival response.

What is surprising in anorexia nervosa is that this normal feedback response is suppressed. In the majority of people, such as the men described in the Ancel Keys' experiment and women who develop bulimia nervosa, even a small degree of weight loss leads to a powerful craving to eat which cannot be ignored. How can people with anorexia nervosa overcome this force? It is possible that one of the genetic vulnerabilities that we consider in Chapter 3 is this ability to override the body's signals. Either these feedback forces are less strong in anorexia nervosa due to a quirk in physiology, or the mental mechanisms which attend to these drives are suppressed. One of the features of recovery is that these counterbalancing forces become reawakened.

Food requirements

In most people appetite is tightly linked to energy expenditure which is reflected in the body's metabolic rate. In anorexia nervosa, metabolic rate is slowed so there is less energy expended at rest. This leads to coldness and fatigue. As soon as food intake is reduced, a clampdown on energy expenditure occurs to minimise the amount of weight loss. In anorexia nervosa, the metabolic rate is increased after recovery, perhaps above normal levels. The mechanism for this is unknown. Perhaps it represents a constitutional tendency to burn off energy more quickly, or it may be that after an episode of anorexia nervosa there is a long period when metabolism is increased to repair the damage caused by the period of starvation.

Hormonal changes also affect metabolism. Women in the second half of their menstrual cycles are metabolically more active, as their bodies prepare for egg implantation. One sign of increased metabolism is the increase in body temperature seen after ovulation.

It is possible to make calculations of the energy needs for an individual, although these do not take into account the genetic and hormonal factors just discussed, but rather give an estimate of average metabolism. The World Health Organisation has produced standard equations (e.g. WHO, 1985), which give a reasonably accurate estimate of maintenance energy requirements in calories per day:

> To gain weight in the face of this basal requirement, 500 extra calories per day are needed to produce a predictable weight gain of 0.5kg per week. The basal metabolic rate needs to be recalculated at various intervals to accounts for the increase in weight ..., change in the degree of starvation, and any change in activity level. Once weight gain has started the basal requirements increase.

Remember this fact when you worry about initially gaining weight after only a small increase in your food.

Sally
Sally and her mother decided to calculate her basal energy requirement. Sally was aged 16 and her weight was 35kg. Although Sally had been exercising rigorously her parents and the school put a stop to this as her level of starvation was severe. When these figures were put into the calculation the daily energy expenditure was 1219kcal.

It is not just the amount eaten that is critical but also the pattern of eating. Regular small meals should be eaten throughout the day. Human physiology has evolved to this style. We are not like the big cats who can gorge once a day or less. We are more like vegetarian mammals who eat small amounts throughout the day. Eating small, frequent meals increases metabolic rate. This means you have to eat more to keep pace, but this pattern is associated with a much better metabolic profile.

- Long gaps between meals signal the body to conserve energy and so any food will be selectively deposited as fat in the expectation of famine. As the balance between fat and lean is disturbed, weight may increase to redress the balance.

- Eating at night has the same effect. At this time the body's hormonal profile promotes storage, in preparation for the fast during sleep.

The pattern of eating can become totally disrupted. Once a conditioned response like this develops it is very difficult to shift, as the rhythm of the body becomes disturbed.

Sharon

Sharon developed anorexia nervosa at the age of 13. She had made a partial recovery but her BMI remained below 17.5. She said she knew that she needed to gain weight, but couldn't. Her sleep pattern became disrupted. She would wake 3–4 times in the night and be driven to get up and eat, otherwise she couldn't get back to sleep. She felt very out of control, eating at night, and her family complained that she disturbed their sleep. She wasn't able to get up in the morning for work. In addition, she felt so guilty about eating at night that she avoided having breakfast.

Sharon's treatment involved gradually shifting her eating pattern. She made a plan to start work in the middle of the day so that at least she would have some structure in her life. She ensured that she had a meal with her mother before she set out for work. Gradually, she set the alarm earlier each morning and introduced breakfast within an hour of getting up and then had a meal before setting out for work. During this time her sleep remained disrupted. She still went to bed but took novels there and did not plan to sleep immediately, just to lie down in good time, warm and comfortable. She was able to reduce gradually the amount she ate at night. Eventually, if she woke at night she did not have to eat before she could fall back to sleep. It took over a year of weight restoration before Sharon was able to sleep throughout the night.

CHANGES THAT OCCUR WHEN THE CLAMP ON DIET IS LIFTED

What happens to weight

The first stage of recovery is very difficult. The pattern of weight gain may not appear to be in step with the changed eating pattern. Weight fluctuations can be large, as glycogen stores in the liver are replenished and packed with water. This rapid rate of weight gain will slowly drop off and more food will be needed to gain weight later.

Also, you may be unlucky and be one of the unfortunate ones to retain fluids. This can lead to large weight swings. In some cases 1–15kg of water accumulates. Vomiting, laxatives or diuretics increase the risk of this happening. One to three months may be needed for the body to re-establish a normal fluid balance. During this time fluid will collect around the eyes overnight and around the ankles at the end of the day. The sensation of bloating and the obvious swelling may act to vindicate your blackest fantasies. The thing you have most feared—uncontrollable weight gain and a visibly bigger body—is happening.

The pattern of fat distribution during weight gain may upset you. You may be sensitive about your stomach becoming bigger. Most of this distension is just an increase of wind and fluid in the sluggish gut.

What happens to the digestive system

The digestive system becomes shrunken and slowed down if food is limited. The gut has to adapt gradually to being stretched and fed again. During this early phase, bloating and abdominal discomfort are common. This is because stomach-emptying is slowed down. Stretching and reconditioning of muscle fibres within the gut walls cause some discomfort. It may take several months for this to subside. Some people become very aware of their stomach distending, particularly after meals. During this early stage you may want to avoid too much roughage, especially the type with insoluble fibre, such as bran, as this may be harder to digest and lead to your gut being overloaded.

Starting to eat

Starting to eat again can be surprisingly difficult. Like any new activity, the best way to start is to get yourself gradually in training rather than to dive in at the deep end. In hospital, if patients are severely underweight we start off on a sloppy, old-fashioned invalid-type diet with scrambled eggs, nutritious soups and milky puddings. The next step is half portions of "normal" food comprising approximately 1250kcal. Again, the food is divided into 3 meals and 3 snacks. As weight is gained it is necessary to increase gradually the amount eaten to maintain a steady increase in weight. The risk of developing bulimia is much lower on a weight-gaining regime like this. We find that bulimia occurs as a complication of anorexia nervosa if the pattern of eating remains abnormal.

It is helpful to develop several strategies to cope with the distress you may experience when you begin to eat again. Some sufferers watch television or listen to the radio during meals, eat with close friends, start writing a novel or directing a film in their heads, carrying the story line from meal to meal, or read something "light" such as a detective story. Here are some examples which have worked for others:

Alex

Alex started to eat after starving himself for eight years. Over the first few weeks he had very painful stomach pains, cramps, bloating and wind. He felt sick, constantly. Nevertheless, he was determined to succeed and persisted. He became very demoralised and frightened when he started to feel hungry. He thought he would never be able to stop eating again. He still persisted and found that this was merely another phase.

Sally

Sally would start a silent argument with herself whenever she felt guilty after eating. She found it easy if she visualised talking to the anorexia minx on her back: "I know it's only you that is making me feel guilty. You are frightened that you are losing your grip on me. You are right. I am determined to pull you off my back. I am putting earplugs in so I can't hear your seductive voice."

Robert

Robert would ensure that he always ate with someone else. When the anorexic attitudes became intense he would concentrate on what his friend was saying. He would encourage his friend to talk about things that had amused him. He even developed a secret code with his friend so that he could flag up quickly that he was feeling tense, and his friend would try to divert him.

Fenolla

Fenolla would use imagery to distract herself from her anorexic thoughts. She would conjure up the image of herself walking away from her anorexic part. She would follow this image on, and construct a daydream in which she was taking part in some adventure. She would take the image and the story from one meal to the next.

The reading list may help you put issues of nutrition and weight and shape into perspective. Some of the books are novels.

FURTHER READING

Barry, J. (1993). *Hungry*. London: Bantam.

Evans-Young, M. (1995). *Dietbreaking*. London: Hodder & Stoughton.

Keys, A.,Brozeck, J., & Henschel, A., Michelson, O., & Taylor, H. (1950). *The biology of human starvation*. Minneapolis, MN: University of Minnesota Press.

Ogden, J. (1992). *Fat chance: The myth of dieting explained*. London: Routledge.

Saunders, T. & Bazalgette, P. (1993). *You don't need to diet*. London: Bantam

Stunkard, A.J. (1988). Some perspectives on human obesity: Its causes. *Bulletin of the New York Academy of Medicine, 64*, 902–938.

WHO (World Health Organisation) (1993). *The ICD-10 classification of mental and behavioral disorders: Diagnostic criteria for research*. Geneva: WHO.

CHAPTER THIRTEEN

Digging deeper: Personality patterns in anorexia nervosa

Certain traits in your personality may have increased your vulnerability to develop anorexia nervosa. We all have underlying patterns of thinking, feeling and behaving, that make up our personality. Some of these patterns we are born with, others are laid down in childhood. There is an interaction between the temperament we are born with, and those of family members and other childhood contacts.

It is useful to digress a little to explain some theories about development, and how we learn to understand the world and, more importantly, the people in it. The developing brain of a child observes events and actions and notes consequences in others and themselves. These are stored as circuits in memory and have been called "schemata". The same child may experience the world very differently if the characteristics of his/her parents differ. For example, if a child with an anxious disposition is brought up by parents with the same characteristics it is likely that the parents will be overprotective. The child will strongly believe that the world is a frightening place and he/she is extremely vulnerable. On the other hand, if the same child is brought up by parents who are bold and do not appear to see dangers, the child may be confused. Their own reactions are not endorsed. They may have difficulty knowing whether they can trust their feelings. This may lead them to feel worthless, guilty and insecure because their view of the world does not match that of their parents. Their reactions are not validated and so they build up somewhat confused schemata.

This adjustment between the temperament of the child and that of the family shifts when the child leaves home, or if the family situation alters. The patterns of behaviour seen in the family no longer hold true. This discrepancy between the actual and the expected pattern can cause trouble. Old patterns of behaviour can become self-defeating, or lead to harm in relationships with others. Despite this, because they are so deeply entrenched and are central to the sense of self, they are very difficult to change.

Schemata which contain pervasive themes regarding oneself and one's relationship with others, and which developed during childhood but are dysfunctional in some way, have been called "early maladaptive schemata". It can be helpful to think of these as having buttons which can get switched on by certain situations and put you into a sort of automatic pilot mode. Problems arise not only in the context of the family but also in the wider cultural setting. Attitudes and expectations for women are a good example of this, and it is probable that these forces together form the development of eating disorders.

When we have these early maladaptive schemata we can react in different ways. We can go on feeling, acting, and behaving as if they were true, or we can over-compensate and act in an opposite way. For example, those who feel they need to be obedient and in control in most situations may be very officious, domineering and authoritarian in other circumstances, perhaps with their dog! Other people go out of their way to avoid triggering their schema as it leads to unpleasant emotions. For example, someone who feels that she is defective will strive to be perfect so that the "failure/not-coming-up-to-scratch schema" is never awakened.

There is a group of personality features or schemata that are characteristic of anorexia nervosa. These include perfectionism, the need for self-discipline or control, the need to please others and a sense of inner defectiveness.

PERFECTIONISM

Many of the behaviour patterns seen in anorexia nervosa reflect an underlying assumption that all love is conditional, that love has to be bought and deserved by effort. It is not freely given. It is as if there is a harsh authority figure who expects high standards of behaviour and/or achievement and/or appearance. It is as if the failure to attain these standards will lead to rejection. This assumption leads to a striving for perfection (see the drawings).

Such a schema may lead to undue deference to authority figures, and a sensitivity to the cultural emphasis on thinness and a healthy diet. Alternatively, perfectionism may take the form of cleanliness and tidiness. Another form may result in the need for academic success or high occupational goals. There is often black-and-white thinking. Events and concepts are judged to be either good or bad, a success or a failure. In some ways this just reflects the cultural stereotyping of women. The children's nursery rhyme of the little girl with the curl, indicates that even as young children, girls are portrayed in extreme ways. Later, the Madonna/Whore split comes into play.

Do you recognise any of these features in yourself? Do you have a highly trained self-critical judge who is quick to chastise and slow to praise?

Look at these drawings. Do they ring any bells with you? Write a list of the thoughts they stir up within you. Do they evoke other images, if so try to get these images down. Do any of these images relate to scenes in childhood? Can you discuss this with your supporter? Do they see any perfectionistic traits within you? With their help perhaps you can notice when this part of you is swinging into action. Keep a diary of how often these thoughts are coming. What terror is it that keeps these thoughts alive and kicking? Is it realistic to think that you would be rejected, unloved and abandoned unless you came up to the grade? Or is it more a fear of being sneered at or humiliated if you get things wrong? Think back to your childhood. Do you have a memory of something like this happening as a child? Did it actually happen or was it implied? Children can be very sensitive to these messages and have no way of judging them against a different standard. Children have a strong need for love and attention so they quickly learn the rules for this to happen. Once you have these schemata implanted in your mind, it takes a great deal of effort to remove them, but it can be done. Discuss with your supporter the terrors you are fleeing. What critical judge are you trying to appease? If a friend of yours, or even your child, believed these schemata, what would you tell them? Can everybody win every competition? How many people can be above average? Is it possible that by always aiming to be perfect it may lead to a continuous demand to be competitive? Others may find this irritating or depressing. They may find it difficult to live with such high standards, or they may not be able to help themselves feeling jealous or envious of your success. They may resent being shown up as lazy or messy. By having such high standards you may be setting yourself up to fail or to become exhausted. Can you take up less competitive activities? Playing with children or doing voluntary work for the disabled are some possibilities.

Try to see yourself more realistically. Accept the rhythm of life. Think about other models of society, rather than a hierarchical tower of power and achievement. Why not try reading books on feminist theories which question this male-dominated model? (See the reading list at the end of this chapter.) We all are mixtures of good and bad, and we will have times when we are full of energy and others when we need to draw in on ourselves. Try to pay attention to the positive aspects of yourself and forgive yourself for your flaws. Can you construct a list of your positive qualities? Perhaps get your supporter to help.

Can you set up little experiments for yourself to test out your perfectionistic rules of living? Plan not to aim for such high standards in one area of your life. Observe what happens. It may be that you are still living in an environment where this view of life holds true, but perhaps not.

Susie

Susie was aged 24. She developed anorexia nervosa at the age of 15. She had one period of inpatient treatment but had failed to gain weight and had quickly relapsed. Her perfectionism took the form of keeping the home clean and tidy. She was the youngest in the family with three older brothers. Her father was somewhat of a perfectionist himself and worked long hours to ensure that his standards were maintained. He had difficulty relaxing at home and would tend to go off to the pub to play darts. Sarah felt that he paid her little attention, apart from her school reports. He was pleased to see that she was successful at school and he encouraged her to persist at this and to obtain the education that he had never enjoyed. She interpreted this as only meriting her father's attention if she attained high standards.

In therapy Susie kept a diary of how often this loop swung into action in her life. She set herself several small experiments in which she gradually tried to decrease her cleaning behaviour. Progress was very slow, she still had strong urges to aim for high standards and her schemata were firmly entrenched. One day, however, she was suddenly able to step outside her narrow patterns of behaviour. She was able to see her behaviour and her habits as an outsider would. Her therapist heard how her urge to clean was so strong that, when a member of her family was eating a snack in the sitting room whilst watching the television, she would be there on the floor with a dustbug hoovering up the crumbs. She began to giggle as she saw the funny side of it. Once this breakthrough had occurred, she was quickly able to stop her perfectionist loop swinging into action as she conjured up that amusing image.

SELF-CONTROL: THE HAIRSHIRT AND OTHER FORMS OF DISCIPLINE

A second common schema in anorexia nervosa involves self-control and discipline (see the drawing over the page). It is as if your own feelings, likes and desires are unacceptable and need to be kept locked away. It is as if you have an uncontrollable needy baby within, which needs to be kept bound and gagged, for fear that it would drain everyone's resources. A high level of control is needed to keep a lid on potentially selfish needs and wishes. This contributes to the ascetic behaviour commonly seen in anorexia nervosa. The seven deadly sins are studiously avoided, and hunger, fatigue, pain, etc., are ignored. Look at the drawing.

How does it make you feel? What thoughts to you have when you see these images? Jot them down.

This type of schema can cause problems when you enter in new relationships in adult life. It is as if you have learnt that a balance of care and affection, need and support is not possible. You may be supportive for others, but it will be difficult for you to accept help and care from them. This may not be a problem in more superficial relationships where people are happy to use your nurturing gifts without giving anything back. You may even be in a job where this is necessary such as nursing. It will cause problems in deeper relationships with equals. Your inability to share your own needs may appear as distancing or as lack of trust. The lack of reciprocity in the relation- ship will lead to your partner feeling uncomfortable. The lack of balance, and of give and take, will make them feel uneasy, selfish or even abusive.

Was there a time in childhood when you felt your needs for attention, care and love were just too much? Was it impossible for you to show any negative emotions as a child? Were feelings of hurt, loss, distress and jealousy dismissed as unacceptable? Can you discuss this with your supporter? If you were confronted now, with yourself as a child, would your needs seem at all unreasonable? Now, as an adult, can you see why your parents were unable to give you what you needed? Can you understand why they found it too difficult to tolerate distress in others?

Penny

Penny was the older of two children. Her father left home when she was 6. Her mother had to go out to work. The children were left in the care of a child minder. The child minder seemed to take a dislike to Penny. She punished her physically and verbally and forced her to be late for school. The child minder's own children and Penny's brother appeared to escape from this animosity. One of the worst aspects of the situation was the unpredictability of the child minder's moods and attacks. Penny kept quiet about all of this. She did not dare tell her mum, as she knew that her mum had to go out to work to make ends meet. She felt that her mum had enough difficulties in her life and didn't want to add to these.

Penny developed anorexia nervosa in her teenage years. She was able to avoid hospitalisation and was even able to keep relationships going, maintaining a bright happy façade. However, when relationships started to become more serious she ran into problems. On two occasions, her partners became uneasy about commitment. In therapy, Penny was able to recognise how difficult it was for her to receive help. She would cancel one out of three sessions. In some ways, she was the perfect patient and would do her homework diligently. However, it was difficult for her to act on any of the solutions that were reached in the therapy sessions. Penny started to keep a diary of the times that she avoided discussing or even thinking of her own needs or actively overriding them. She then began to try to let her husband help. For example, she let him prepare her breakfast each day and eat it with her. Over time, their relationship gradually improved.

If you have a strong control schema, you will need to develop skills to attend to your own emotions, which are markers of your needs. One of the first steps will be to understand what emotions are and how they affect us. Some of these emotions will be painful and distressing. You may have been able to put these aside or ignore them by starving but this tends to just put them on hold rather than deal with them effectively. You cannot avoid the work that needs to be done to process emotions. For example, if you have lost someone who was important to you, it is crucial to go through the pain and difficulty of grieving. If you attempt to short-circuit it, it will only pop up again later. A good example of the amount of painful work that is necessary in grieving is seen in Susan Hill's book *In the summertime of the year.*

Painful and distressing emotions are part of life. They cannot be banished. Although they can feel overwhelming, it is helpful to develop coping strategies. You will be able to tolerate them. They are not disgusting or sinful.

In order to recover from anorexia nervosa new skills need to be developed, especially those related to emotion regulation. You need to know that you don't have to try to avoid negative emotions in order to cope. You will be able to master unpleasant emotions with techniques such as self-soothing and acceptance. These are the sorts of issues that you may want to deal with in counselling, or with your friend:

1. Understand the emotions you experience.
   (a) Identify the emotions.
   (b) Understand what emotions do for you.
2. Reduce your emotional vulnerability.
   (a) Decrease negative vulnerability.
   (b) Increase positive emotions.
3. Decrease emotional suffering.
   (a) Let go of painful emotions through mindfulness.
   (b) Change painful emotions through opposite action.

A good way to approach this is to think of ways of soothing your five senses (it is all right if you exclude the sense of taste!). Examples are:

Vision: Buy a flower, go to an art gallery, light a candle.
Hearing: Listen to music, sing a song (what about "My favourite things" from *The Sound of Music*).
Smell: Use your favourite perfume or try some scents in a shop. Use some of the techniques of aromatherapy.
Touch: Have a bubble bath, stroke a pet, have a massage, soak your feet.
Taste: You may even be able to enjoy this one at some future date!

PLEASING BEHAVIOUR

Another common schema in anorexia nervosa leads sufferers to act as if they are worthless or defective. To compensate for and hide this inner badness, there is a strong drive to please. Sufferers can behave like doormats, letting others tread on them. Look at the drawing, how does it make you feel?

In some cases, the feeling of worthlessness in relationship to others can alternate with its opposite, a feeling of superiority. You may be contemptuous of others who spend so much energy and time on eating. It is difficult to find the balance between feeling looked down on and trampled underfoot, or looking down on others.

If you think back to your childhood, were there any times when you felt a strong drive to please? Did your position in the family mean that you only got noticed if you joined up with someone else?

If you suppress your own needs and wishes in order to please others you end up becoming furiously angry. Unless you are an Oscar-winning actress it will be difficult not to let this resentment show. It can be very

disconcerting for others to have a seemingly compliant and easy-going person become transformed into a "vitriolic harridan". If you always say "yes" it is difficult for others to see you as a person. It is almost as if you become an automaton.

Hannah

Hannah was the youngest in a family of three. She followed her older sister to boarding school. Her sister had been a star pupil and became head girl. Hannah turned away from academic pursuits and instead aimed to be liked by her school friends. She became the class joker. She could always be relied on to be in mischief, and to took the role of the naughtiest in the class. She had difficulty in settling to any career or training after school. Within a year she accidentally became pregnant. It had not crossed her mind to think about contraception. She arranged a termination and told one or two close friends. She was unable to tell her parents and the next day when she returned home she had to join in a game of tennis with her family and friends as if nothing had happened.

Her illness began after she returned from a trip to New Zealand with a girlfriend. On her return to London this same girlfriend became involved in a relationship and cut her off. This was one of the stressful events that preceded her anorexia.

A major issue in Hannah's therapy was the recognition of this tendency to please others, rather than thinking what she would like for herself. She started to keep a diary of when these events occurred. In sessions she practised role-playing some of these scenarios in a more assertive manner. Little by little she was able to change her interactions with friends. However, progress was slow and there was the tendency to slip back. For example, when her therapy stopped and she went away to university she became involved in a relationship with a man who was highly regarded in her set as "cool", but who walked all over her. Hannah's eating deteriorated and she lost weight. However, by the time she had come back for a follow-up session she was able to recognise what had happened and had ended the relationship.

One of the first steps in dealing with the pleasing "trap" is to identify and express your own preferences and natural inclinations. Women have lived in a male-dominated environment for many years. They have adapted to this powerless position by behaving passively, or obtaining what they want by indirect "manipulative" ways. It is sometimes difficult for women to acknowledge their preferences. You may need to develop assertiveness skills. There are many classes and books on this and you may need to try several in order to find one which suits you. A good book to start with is *A woman in your own right* by A. Dickson.

Many women lack confidence in using assertiveness. You will need to learn how to balance priorities versus demands, wants versus shoulds. Many women see assertiveness as an aggressive response, or any expression of their own needs as selfishness. There is a wide open space of middle ground between passivity and aggression, and between selflessness and selfishness. You can develop an appropriate degree of assertion and self-nurturance. You need to work on what goals are appropriate for you. Often, this can be complex and requires you to balance your needs with the needs of others and your own moral principles. You will need to learn to give and take and use negotiation skills.

INNER DEFECTIVENESS

One of the schemata which may lie behind the need to please and to be perfect is the inner convictions that somehow one is defective. "No one would like me if they knew the real me." "When people like me I feel I am fooling them." Do these ring true for you?

How does this image make you feel? Does it bring to mind other images? Have there been times when people have expressed their disgust or criticism of you? Were there times when this happened as a child? Were there times when you were made to feel ashamed, criticised or humiliated? Would you be able to discuss some of these images with your counsellor/ friend? Does your friend think it appropriate that you were treated in this way as a child? What would your friend say if she saw someone talking like this to her child? Did your friend get criticised in a similar way?

These personality features or schemata are contributing factors that keep the anorexic behaviour going. The need to achieve weight loss can quickly tap into the perfectionist schema. Which leads to the idea of having the ideal shape to fit with society's expectations. The need to control one's own impulses and drives becomes transformed into the need to control hunger. Low self-esteem/inner defectiveness can be masked if your outer shell is acceptable to society. The extreme effect of some of these positions makes the opposite appear terrifying and so any shift becomes difficult.

FURTHER READING

Hill, S. (1986). *In the summertime of the year*. Harmondsworth, UK: Penguin.

Feminist texts

Baker-Miller, J. (1978). *Towards a new psychology of women*. Harmondsworth, UK: Penguin.

Berlotti, E. (1977). *Little girls*. London: Readers & Writers Co-operative.

Daly, M.(1986). *Beyond God the Father*. London: Women's Press

De Beauvoir, S. (1960). *The second sex*. London: Jonathan Cape.

Dickson, A. (1982). *A woman in your own right*. London: Quartet.

English, D., & Ehrenreich, B. (1979). *For her own good*. London: Pluto.

Forisba, B. (1981). Feminist therapy. In R.Corsini (Ed.), *Handbook of innovative therapies*. New York: Wiley.

Friedan, B. (1977). *The feminine mystique*. New York: Dell.

Gimbutas, M. (1982). *The goddesses and gods of old Europe*. London: Thames & Hudson.

Greer, G. (1971). *The female eunuch*. London: Paladin.

Hall, N. (1980). *The moon and the virgin*. London: Women's Press.

Orbach, S., & Eichenbaum, L. (1983). *What do women want?* London: Pelican

Orbach, S.,& Eichenbaum, L. (1985). *Understanding women*. London: Pelican.

Perara, S. (1981). *Descent to the goddess*. Toronto: Inner City Books.

Stone, M. (1976). *When God was a woman*. New York: Harcourt Brace Jovanovich

CHAPTER FOURTEEN

Repeating patterns

As we discussed in Chapter 3, there is a genetic vulnerability to develop anorexia nervosa. Female relatives are at most risk and the risk is higher in our current cultural climate. Thus, it is not uncommon for two sisters to have an eating disorder. One out of fourteen families will have another family member affected. This causes additional difficulties.

If the mother is also affected, mealtimes are much more complex. It may be that mother has never eaten with the family, or if she has, she has always eaten different meals. A mother's preoccupation with shape and weight may be directly transferred on to her daughter. We saw in Chapter 2 how Clare had a mother who, although she did not have an eating disorder, set very high standards for her daughter's appearance and eating patterns. We can easily understand how this may develop in our present culture of thinness. Parents of a fat child are often criticised as not caring enough. However, as indicated in Chapter 3, weight may be under strong genetic control, with some people gaining weight much more easily than others. Also, there are phases in childhood and development, just around puberty, when a certain amount of "puppy fat" is normal. The increase in fat in females is related to the ability to have children.

Margaret

Margaret was an Anglo-Indian girl who was adopted at the age of 1 year into a white middle class family in which there were two older sons. A younger boy was also adopted two years later. From the age of 9 her mother became preoccupied with the weight of her two adopted children. She had a weight chart in the kitchen. They had different meals to the rest of the family and were forbidden to have second helpings and their lunch packs were spartan. Margaret compensated for this by stealing money from her mother's purse and buying snacks and sweets away from home. Her friends at school also shared their food with her. From the age of 14 Margaret developed an eating disorder which varied between severe restriction and bingeing.

In other cases, the mother may have bent over backwards to prevent her own attitudes to shape and weight affecting her child and yet may be horrified to see her daughter developing anorexic tendencies.

Rachel

Rachel's mother had developed anorexia nervosa before her marriage. She recovered and had Rachel, but suffered a relapse after her birth. She went for infertility treatment and had twins several years later. Her anorexia nervosa persisted but was not medically severe and she never had treatment.

Rachel started to develop anorexia nervosa at the age of 13 in the context of bullying at school. Her mother thought that the family should eat together but mealtimes became more and more stressful occasions. Rachel always felt that her mother was putting too much food on her plate. She sensed that there was competition and rivalry between them. She thought that her mother wanted to make her fat. On the other hand, Rachel's mother was only too aware of how anorexia had nearly destroyed her own life. She likened it to a heroin fix, and she did not want her daughter's life to be maimed by the illness.

Rachel's parents discussed this problem. They agreed to accept that family mealtimes would not have a rigid structure in their house. Rather they had a routine pre-meal get-together when they had a drink and discussed the events of the day while preparing their meals within the kitchen. The decision where and with whom to eat was left flexible. Rachel's mother went to see the school nurse and explained that she was concerned that Rachel might have anorexia nervosa. The school nurse offered to weigh Rachel each week and to ensure that Rachel went to the dining room to eat her packed lunch. Rachel and the nurse agreed that the nurse would let her mother know if her weight continued to fall, as her mother would need to get further help or think of another solution.

If you have, or have had, anorexia nervosa and you are aware that your daughter is developing signs, it is important to share your concerns with someone else. It may be helpful to be frank, and acknowledge that you may have a blind or over-sensitive spot because of your own difficulties, and that you need more impartial help. The fact that there is an increased genetic risk does not mean that nothing can be done about it. The environment accounts for at least 50% of the risk. In addition, the genetic vulnerability may need some sort of environmental, psychological or social stress before it expresses itself. You can do your best to ensure that the family environment is as supportive as possible and ensure that some of the more harmful cultural influences are modified by the family.

CHAPTER FIFTEEN

Recovery

It is important to discuss the topic of recovery. I am often asked: "Will I ever get over it?". Many people have unrealistic expectations and think that the illness will go after a few months. I am afraid you need to think in terms of years rather than months. Clinically, it is often said that one cannot predict the outcome until five years have passed.

After five years, approximately half the population with anorexia nervosa will have recovered; 30% will remain quite severely affected by their illness; and 20% will still be underweight and without their periods.

What about the recovered group? Have they totally got over all their symptoms?

It is unusual to see somebody who has totally shaken off all their abnormal attitudes to food and eating. Perhaps this is not surprising as anorexic attitudes to food and eating merge into Western cultural attitudes about health and attractiveness. I have met people at a normal weight 20 years after their illness, who are still quite preoccupied with weight and shape. They say things like: "If it wasn't for my husband and children I know I would start losing weight again."

Even after a 2 to 3-year period of recovery, relapse does occur. Relapse particularly occurs after stressful events, or if weight loss has been triggered by any reason. For example, after childbirth, the increased stress of looking after a new child, combined with the weight changes after birth, can lead to a relapse. However, people are often aware of the danger signs and can stop the illness getting a severe grip on them. It is perhaps important to consider anorexia nervosa as an Achilles' heel that will return at times of stress.

Other people continue to have rather rigid eating habits and never eat as much or as freely as others.

What happens to those who haven't recovered by five years?

People who have struggled with the illness for longer than five years can still shake it off. The habit has been much more firmly entrenched and so it is much more difficult, but we have seen recovery after 20–30 years of illness. It is never too late, and no one should ever give up hope.

It may be necessary to change the goals for recovery. We discussed earlier that, in some cases, to expect full recovery after a long illness is not realistic. Even partial weight recovery can be of value in that it means continuing hospital admissions are not necessary and health is improved. On the other hand, if you continue to suffer from a severe form of anorexia nervosa, the health risk increases.

Unfortunately, in specialist treatment centres we mainly just see forms of anorexia nervosa which are severe enough to need hospital treatment. We are aware that there are many cases that occur and which recover with help from parents, teachers and family doctors. It is therefore possible that our view of the natural course of the illness is rather *skewed* towards pessimism. There is a strong clinical impression that if the illness is treated early enough, recovery is greatly improved.

What are the factors that affect recovery?

These are quite logical and simple:

1. *Severity of the anorexia nervosa*
   - The more weight that has been lost and the more extreme the emaciation the worse is the outcome.
   - The longer the illness has gone on before treatment starts.
   - If the illness has failed to respond to several attempts at treatment.
2. *Background vulnerability*
   - The other factors associated with a poorer prognosis are those that indicate problems in adjustment during childhood, before the anorexia began.
   - Childhood problems, such as school refusal and emotional problems.
   - Difficulty in making friends, severe shyness or alienation.
   - Difficulties within the family.

Listing the facts about recovery can seem rather turgid. It can be more interesting to listen to how other people have struggled and overcome their illness. There is no set pattern. The stories vary considerably.

Miriam

Miriam had been ill for five years and had been in and out of hospital on several occasions. She failed to gain weight even in hospital. Her relatives were extremely concerned about her and had brought her to another clinic. Miriam was told that they expected her to work on her problems as an outpatient. She was rather surprised at this as she felt that she needed inpatient treatment. She felt very unmotivated to start to fight her anorexia nervosa. Her weight during the initial four sessions remained extremely low and her therapist remained extremely anxious about her. She had to give up work as she had fainted on several occasions. Her general practitioner had been so concerned about her physical state that she was admitted to a local hospital, but she discharged herself within a day. Eventually, after 8 or 10 sessions, Miriam became more engaged in treatment, she was able to open up about the underlying problems associated with her illness. Her perfectionism for instance, meant that she spent most of the day cleaning the house. Her illness meant that she had a lot of control over the family. Her mother couldn't use the kitchen as Miriam regarded it as her territory. She would determine what other people could have, make the tea and keep it clean and tidy. One breakthrough in treatment was when she was able to see these underlying patterns of behaviour from an outside perspective. She also realised that it was up to her to start and work on her problems. No magic solution would be found by entering hospital, or from therapy alone.

Miriam woke up one morning deciding that she was going to tackle her illness. She enlisted her mother's help and gradually increased what she was eating, and allowing her weight to rise slowly. With her weight gain Miriam regained her remarkable sense of humour. She had always described the teasing repartee that went on in the household, but now Miriam herself was a major player in this. She started to bicycle, got a job and was able to resume former friendships.

Nicola

Nicola had had anorexia nervosa for 15 years. She had been in and out of hospital on 10 or more occasions. Often, she had been treated under the Mental Health Act. She had reached the stage where she had had to have a tube directly into her stomach for refeeding. After this very severe episode, her brother became more involved with her. He said that he was going to help her get over her illness. He spent some time talking with her and introducing her to his friends. Her brother was very interested in "working-out" and he took Nicola to the gym where she became interested in step aerobics. Nicola's general practitioner arranged for her to have psychotherapy in a specialist unit. In psychotherapy, she was able to understand how her patterns of behaviour and expectations had fitted in with the anorexia nervosa. She was able to maintain a normal eating pattern. She became extremely involved in the step aerobics, progressing to be a tutor and trainer. After five years of unemployment she was able to resume her old job of teaching. Nicola described how her brother's warmth and concern had enabled her to start to believe that she could recover from the illness.

Mary

Mary had had the illness for 20 years. Her husband was a general practitioner, as was Mary herself. Mary had seen many other specialists, gastroenterologists and endocrinologists about her symptoms. She and her husband remained convinced that she had some medical illness which made her lose weight. Eventually, Mary's own general practitioner referred her to a specialist unit. Mary attended regularly and worked hard at trying to overcome her illness. However, she felt very stuck and was unable to change. She had read about fluoxetine being used in anorexia nervosa and was interested in giving it a try. (Fluoxetine is a drug that has been mainly used for depression, but also in bulimia nervosa. It has not been fully tested in anorexia nervosa and remains slightly experimental at the present time. Doctors have been interested in its use in anorexia nervosa as it can be helpful for the compulsive obsessions and compulsions that can co-occur.) Mary found that she became much calmer on the tablets. She found that she needed far more sleep. She would sleep normally, take her children to school and then go back to bed and sleep for several hours in the morning. She noted that she was able to sit down and be more relaxed within the home. She describes in the past never being able to sit and watch the television with her children, she was always driven to some activity. This was now possible and she was able to let her children have more freedom. She found that she still remained extremely concerned about her weight, for example, even when she came to the clinic she would never want to see her weight.

She remained frightened of evidence that her weight was increasing. Nevertheless, she was able to eat a little more, although the content of her diet remained far from normal.

Other positive benefits were that she became much stronger physically. Looking after the children was easier, she was able to be less strict and controlling and was able to enjoy them more. A welcome change was to sit and cuddle them. She was also able to treat herself better. She was able to buy herself new clothes and could set limits on other people's demands.

It is important to note that Mary's case is not typical. The effects of fluoxetine are rather idiosyncratic. It does not appear to affect the core anorexic symptoms but it can help with the illness. However, we need to wait until controlled clinical trials have taken place so that we can evaluate whether the risks involved in taking this drug are outweighed by any benefits. In the United States, however, fluoxetine is used in anorexia nervosa more widely than in the United Kingdom.

Pauline
Pauline came to a specialist unit after a crisis referral from her local psychiatric services. She had gone for help when she had been unable to climb the stairs at work. When she presented, she had a severe weakness of the thigh muscles. She had also lost the function of one of the nerves to the foot and so her foot was dragging when she was walking. She was slightly surprised at all the fuss as she had not noticed anything wrong.

At university, there was a period where she had lost weight. She had counselling and had gained weight and fully recovered. Later, she was made redundant, and was let down in a love affair. She found another job but had become very concerned about eating with others at lunchtime. She felt that she had nothing to contribute to the conversation, and she therefore skipped lunch. In the evening she spent a lot of time preparing her food, which was mainly vegetables and fruit.

She was shocked when the specialist psychiatrist pointed out the severity of her illness and described the medical dangers to her. She was advised that inpatient treatment was probably necessary. It was agreed that she could stay at home but only if she could ensure that someone would be there to look after her. She asked her father to stay with her, and he travelled several hundred miles to be with her. She was asked to come again in two days time with her father. She and her father made a plan whereby she would eat every few hours. She was able to stick to this and gradually she gained weight with treatment. She said that recognising her dangerous condition had enabled her to work on it.

Karen

Karen is 27 years old. She is the only daughter of two academics. She has one older brother who was considered very bright. Her mother is of Central European origin and, although Karen had grown up in the United Kingdom her family had remained quite isolated, pursuing high academic standards. Karen felt that she could not talk to her mother, who always put the brother first, whereas Karen was "daddy's little girl". She developed anorexia nervosa during her A-level year, saying she wanted control over her life, as she felt her parents were ruling it for her. On leaving school she nevertheless obtained a place in college but had difficulty in making friends and felt that she did not fit in. She subsequently left and obtained a job in the Civil Service where she has remained ever since. Her anorexia nervosa waxed and waned over this 10-year period and she had many different forms of treatment, ranging from hypnotherapy to psychoanalytic psychotherapy. She was finally admitted to hospital for the first time, aged 26. She attributed her recovery to this period of inpatient treatment, as she felt she was unable to do it "on my own". Treatment included family therapy and Karen found herself better able to relate to her mother on an adult level. She remains well a year following discharge with one minor relapse during a period of depression, which was arrested as soon as she realised it was happening.

Jackie

Jackie is 25. She is a student nurse who had never been concerned with her weight or shape until the break-up of a relationship in which she felt betrayed. She initially lost her appetite which resulted in weight loss. During this period she was able to confide in her friends, but later began to feel she was boring them. They noticed that she had lost a lot of weight and looked ill, and were concerned. Later, her weight plummeted and she was referred for outpatient psychotherapy. It was during this period that she describes crossing a common on a sunny summer's day and she suddenly realised that the only reason she was miserable was solely because she was not allowing herself to eat, and says that her recovery began from that episode. She gradually regained weight, her periods returned and she has remained well since.

FURTHER READING

Other people have written about their experiences of recovery. For example:

MacLeod, S. (1983) *The art of starvation*. Harmondsworth, UK: Virago.

Wilkinson, H. (1984). *Puppet on a string*. London: Hodder & Stoughton.

SECTION FOUR

Guidelines for professionals

CHAPTER SIXTEEN

Guidelines for therapists/carers

The concept of this book arose out of our experience of writing a self-help book for bulimia nervosa *Getting better bit(e) by bit(e)* (Schmidt & Treasure, 1993). Although it seemed simple to write a sister volume for anorexia nervosa I soon realised that the situation was much more complex. Bulimia nervosa is a secret condition in which others are rarely involved. In contrast, the problem in anorexia nervosa is overt, anyone can make a "spot diagnosis". Also, one of the key features in anorexia nervosa is the fact that the sufferer herself doesn't think she has a problem. This feature was noted in the earliest cases (see Chapter 4). In the past, this has been termed "denial"; I now prefer to label this as the "precontemplation" stage of the process of change. Therefore, it is common to have the woman with anorexia nervosa blithely unconcerned as she becomes sicker and sicker while everyone around her frets and panics and gets sucked into her orbit.

The concept of a self-help book therefore had to change. I thought that a model of guided-self-change would be more appropriate. I therefore tackled this problem in two ways. First, I wrote a section for family members. I then tried to structure the book using the transtheoretical model of change of Prochaska and DiClemente (1986). This book is therefore designed to be a resource suitable for clients at all stages of motivation.

I hope that you will find this book of use to you as a therapist. However, it will not give you all the skills and knowledge that you need to deal with complex cases. (I am writing a companion book which aims to answer those needs.) If you are a trained counsellor you should find that this book is useful for cases which have presented early in the course of their illness. It will help you guide the sufferer and her family through some of the early stages.

FIRST PRINCIPLES

There are a few principles that you should note before you begin therapy. It is important, before you start to work with someone with an eating disorder, that you arrange a medical assessment to confirm the diagnosis, to rule out other medical conditions and to assess the severity of the illness. Further medical assessments will be necessary if weight loss continues or if physical problems arise.

I cannot stress enough the need for you to regularly monitor weight. I suggest that it is best if you do this yourself. It is an important part of the therapeutic relationship. It is the opportunity for your client to tell you how things have been going. She may be reluctant to displease you by telling you openly that she has difficulties. She may fear criticism and rejection and try to cover up any failings. The weight scales will allow her to be honest. If you don't have scales then arrange for an accurate weight to be recorded and given to you. The practice nurse at the general practitioner's surgery may be able to help. Not only should you measure weight but you should also plot it on a graph so that you can clearly see any time trends. If the weight is progressively falling it is a clear signal that therapy is not being effective and you need to obtain help and/or arrange for a transfer into a more specialist setting. If weight is increasing, no matter how slowly then that is a sign that your therapy is effective and you can continue. If you are stuck and weight remains static then it is a good idea to arrange for a second opinion or a consultation.

Of course, we can all be deceived by measures to alter weight falsely, such as drinking large amounts of fluid before the consultation, putting weights in clothes, etc. Therefore, it is also important to develop good clinical judgement and be alert to any symptoms or signs that all is not going well. A simple measure, such as measuring the pulse rate or the blood pressure, can be very informative. A very slow heart rate less than 55bpm (beats per minute), or a low blood pressure, less than 85/60mmttg (millimetres of mercury), is a cause for concern. Remember that anorexia nervosa has a mortality level twice that of any other illness and so you must make sure your procedure is safe. Do not be afraid to ask for help. Expressing and acknowledging your concern and your need to involve others is good practice and will help to model appropriate behaviour for your client. One of the key maladaptive coping behaviours in anorexia nervosa is that sufferers avoid facing their problems and do not open up to others. Do not be drawn into this pattern of behaviour. The following are important danger signs: they indicate that starvation has reached a critical level and that you quickly need medical help.

1. Thigh and shoulder weakness which makes climbing stairs or brushing hair difficult.
2. Faints or dizziness on getting up suddenly.
3. Fits (episodes when consciousness is lost associated with muscle-jerking).
4. Episodes of light-headedness or panic, with palpitations.
5. Measles-like rash on the skin.
6. Breathlessness.
7. Severe exhaustion.
8. Extremely cold and blue toes.

These signs are markers that indicate that starvation is severe. They must not be ignored. Weight loss of this degree of severity usually requires urgent hospital admission. There may also be more "silent" dangers which are only revealed by blood tests. Any "funny turns" in anorexia nervosa need to be taken seriously as they may be the signals of later serious problems.

You can test muscle power by asking your client to crouch down on her haunches. Can she get up from this position without using her arms for leverage? If not, this is a sign that muscle function is severely impaired. *You must arrange an urgent assessment with a view to admission immediately.* The state of the circulation can be assessed by looking at toes, fingers and nose. Cold, blue mottling indicates that the peripheral circulation is poor.

CHOOSING A MANAGEMENT PLAN

How you manage the case will depend upon your client's age and the age at which the anorexia developed. It is obvious that the family of the younger client will need to be seen as they will be automatically involved in the problem. Also, if the illness developed early in life and your client is still living at home she will in many ways be functioning at the age level at which the anorexia began. Her maturation will be stunted. For example, you may have a case in which the illness began at the age of 11, she remains prepubertal physically and her mental development will also remain childlike in terms of abstract concepts. Although she is now 24 it will still be important to involve the family in management. Research has found that family education and counselling is probably more effective than family therapy and is more acceptable.

The family may feel frightened, guilty and confused as to what to do. Work with this book as a resource to give them information. They may find it helpful to go over Chapters 2 and 3 so that they can understand what the illness is about and what may have contributed to its development.

Anorexia nervosa has a long time course, five years on average. It is difficult to cope with the anxiety and frustration that living at close-quarters with this problem can bring. Emotions such as anger, criticism or the converse, coolness and distancing can also arise. Unfortunately, these only serve to stoke the fires of the illness. As a therapist, it is helpful if you foster a warm, caring relationship within the family. Try to reframe worries and concerns into positive features. If, despite the best of your efforts, the family remains hostile and critical to the sufferer you will need to sideline their involvement as much as possible. It may be helpful to suggest that the family join a carers' support group. Realising that other families have the same problem and that it is the illness rather than their daughter's stubbornness or wilfulness can help defuse the tension. Working through Chapters 5 and 6 may help with this. The only feature that marks anorexic families out from any others is the finding that they are weak on effective problem-solving. It may therefore be useful to coach them in the techniques of problem-solving that are outlined in Chapter 6. Start off with simple tasks and gradually guide them upwards.

With older clients, you will spend more time working with them individually, although do not be afraid to recruit members of the family to help whenever you and the client think it is necessary, and especially if you are stuck or failing in therapy as evidenced by the weight chart. Working with your client on the exercises detailed in Chapter 9 can be very important.

CRITICAL POINTS

- Work in close conjunction with someone who can give you a medical evaluation before and during your work.
- Weigh your client regularly.
- Chart the weight and use it as the basis of a collaborative relationship with your client.

- Communicate regularly with others involved: the general practitioner, the referring agency, members of your team.
- Get help if weight continues to fall.
- Ask for a second opinion or consultation if the weight remains static.
- Be alert for medical danger signs and symptoms.
- Involve the family at an age-appropriate level.
- Be sensitive to the demoralisation and frustration that living with a chronic stigmatising illness can bring.
- Be a resource of information.
- Offer skills training, especially in problem-solving, for the family.

FURTHER READING

Prochaska, J.O., DiClemente, C.C., & Norcross, J.C. (1992). In search of how people change: Applications to addictive behaviors. *American Psychologist, 47*, 1102–1114.

CHAPTER SEVENTEEN

Guidelines for teachers

As a teacher you are in a prime position to notice if a pupil is developing anorexia nervosa.

1. In games you may spot that a child has lost weight.
2. In young children (before puberty is completed) you may observe a child not gaining height relative to the rest of the class because her growth has been impaired.
3. A pupil who was previously socially active may become withdrawn and sad.
4. Instead of going out to the playground the student will cling to the radiators to keep warm or wear numerous layers of clothes to fight off the cold.
5. The pupil may avoid the company of others in order to run around the sports field or do some other form of exercise.
6. The sufferer may skip school meals or eat only fruits and vegetables.

Schools can also implement a structure which will help overcome the anorexia.

It is helpful if one teacher takes the key role. Ideally, this is the teacher who gets on best with the sufferer. The form teacher or a pastoral tutor may be appropriate.

Once the problem has been recognised the next step is to share your concerns with the parents. You will be able to develop a collaborative relationship in which you plan to meet together on a regular basis to assess progress.

WHAT CAN THE SCHOOL DO?

Jointly with the parents the school can set limits and boundaries to prevent the anorexic behaviour taking over.

Exercise
Exercise at school should be stopped. This will include activities in the timetable and the extra activity undertaken in free time. It is easy to justify this, as exercise at low weight poses a great risk to health. It is not appropriate to expect the school to accept this risk.

Mealtimes
It is important to have a carefully thought out plan of action and to keep it under review. It makes sense to have a number of options available and choose whichever seems appropriate, or change according to progress. Possible options include:

1. Eating as normal with the other pupils.
2. Recruiting a friend to be a minder to sit with her and make sure that the meal gets eaten.
3. Eating with a member of staff.
4. Eating in a separate room.
5. Eating at the staff table.
6. Eating away from the main dining area but with a minder/friend.

Options 3–5 should be considered with caution, however, as they could lead to further social alienation of the sufferer. A similar policy should be adopted about snacks. Snacks in the form of a milky drink and sandwich are ideal. The eating plan should include regular small meals throughout the day.

Homework
The perfectionist traits common in anorexia nervosa mean that homework assignments can take far longer than is reasonable. Teachers can work with parents to set a suitable time limit for study.

Examinations

Anorexia nervosa interferes with concentration and cognitive function. It may be helpful to provide the examination authorities with a letter from a doctor explaining the illness (in the case of important public examinations). It may be necessary to ensure that there is a break during the exam for a hot drink and snack. Sufferers may be troubled by cold, as examinations involve sitting still for long periods, and remedial action such as a blanket or hot water bottle may help.

Career advice

Often, women who develop anorexia nervosa do very well academically. This is partly a result of their innate ability, but also arises because their perfectionist traits lead them to strive harder. These traits mean that they thrive very well in the structured environment of school. On the other hand, these same trends can lead to misery in an unstructured course with no guidelines about what is expected and no clear feedback. A university course with few lectures and little practical work, such as English and History, can be very difficult.

Starvation draws people towards food-related careers. This was clearly seen in the American Ancel Keys' experiment referred to earlier, in which several of the men turned towards careers in the food industry when the experiment was over. There is no clear evidence whether this is a good or bad thing.

Careers closed to sufferers

You may be precluded from training as a dietician if you have anorexia nervosa. A government enquiry following the case of Beverly Allit (a nurse who killed young children in her care) led to the Clothier Report. This report makes recommendations to occupational health physicians who work in medical settings. It suggests that students should not be accepted into training for the health professions if they are suffering from an eating disorder. They advise that there should be a period of two years' recovery with no therapeutic input, before training begins.

However, a recent report from the Department of Health has indicated that this recommendation is not reasonable.

CHAPTER EIGHTEEN

The family doctor's perspective

The classical case of anorexia nervosa is not hard to diagnose. However, it may be difficult to elicit all the symptoms as the sufferer may be unforthcoming. She may have been brought to the clinic reluctantly. She may say she has no worries about her weight loss and that her parents are making a fuss. Do not fall into the trap of arguing with her. Listen to her then ask questions such as: "Why are your parents worried?" "What exactly are they worried about?" "Are you able to join in with your friends as easily as before?" "Have you been troubled by feeling the cold?" It is important to take the parents' concerns seriously and not be fobbed off by the hostile girl being somewhat unforthcoming.

You can make the diagnosis if the following are present:

1. *Weight loss in the absence of organic illness*. (If the parents give a coherent history of self-induced weight loss further investigation to rule out other causes of weight reduction is unnecessary.) Atypical presentations do occur in which the explanation of why eating is difficult is a vaguely defined abdominal distress. In these cases further investigation may be needed. Failure to grow rather than a loss of weight occurs in prepubertal children.

2. *Amenorrhoea*. (This may be absent if the patient is taking the contraceptive pill. In males, the equivalent hormonal marker is loss of early morning erections. Obviously, these signs are not present in prepubertal children.)

3. *Distorted body image*. Patients may say they feel fat even though they are underweight. (This is not always present. Some patients will say that they know they are thin but they cannot do anything about it.) Also, patients may say they are terrified of gaining weight.

ATYPICAL PRESENTATION

Making the diagnosis can be difficult in atypical presentations, such as individuals younger or older than average, and in males.

Children: Anorexia nervosa occurs in children as young as 7 years of age. There is a greater proportion of males in the younger age group (young Male:Female 1:3 vs adolescent M:F 1:10). Children this age may not be able to articulate the reasons why they have lost weight. The diagnosis can be inferred from their behaviour. Reserves of fat are lower in children, and starvation quickly impairs basic physiological function. Peripheral circulatory failure can lead to ischaemic changes in the toes causing gangrene.

Males: Excessive exercise rather than extreme food restriction may be the way that anorexia nervosa presents in males. Rather than stating that they want to lose weight, the explanation for the exercise may be that they wish to become fit or do not want to be lazy.

Older women: Older women (over 30) can develop a syndrome of extreme weight loss with pronounced depressive features. They can usually provide no explanation for their weight reduction, but family members observe that they eat very little. Sufferers will deny that they want to be thinner and say they are trying to gain weight. However, the attitude to food and eating is frequently distorted. Often these women have had to face severe stress such as the loss of close family members. Disentangling the features of depression from those of anorexia nervosa can be difficult. However, the depressive features do not respond to antidepressants when patients are at a low weight.

WHAT CAN BE DONE IN PRIMARY CARE

Early cases can be managed in primary care (Myers et al., 1993). Some cases require a much briefer intervention than that described in Chapter 16. The practice nurse can be an invaluable source of help and support and can monitor the weight regularly.

Referral to a specialist centre may be necessary if short-term interventions have been unsuccessful.

FURTHER READING

Myers, S., Treasure, J., & Davies, M. (1993). *A general practitioner's guide to eating disorders*. A Maudsley Practical Handbook (sponsored by Boots Pharmaceuticals Ltd.).